Life by Design

A Personal Plan for Bringing Out the Best in Yourself

Dr. Rick Brinkman

&

Dr. Rick Kirschner

Library of Congress Catalog Card Number: 99-70739

First edition published by McGraw-Hill 1999

Second edition published by Rick Brinkman Productions, 2012

Dr. Rick Brinkman performs keynote speeches and trainings.

For more resources visit:

www.rickbrinkman.com or call 503-635-4145

dr.rick@rickbrinkman.com

Dedicated to the creators of good in the world to be,
may tomorrow be your best,
and tomorrow better than today.

ACKNOWLEDGEMENTS

Thanks to our parents, Simone & Felix Brinkman, Alan & Lois Kirschner, who gave us life and inspired us to live it by design; to our wives Lisa and Lindea, for their constant love, insight and inspiration; to our daughters Carle and Aden, who will inherit the future of these endeavors; to our network of family and friends who give us reason to believe in a brighter future for humanity; to Jaime for his clarity; to Bucky, you're the trimtab; to licensed naturopathic physicians who use the principles of nature to light the path to health.

TABLE OF CONTENTS

tion and momentum.

verse of support.

20. Loving For Life   197

Part 5 Choices About The World   209
21. Knowing The World   211

22. Owning The World   221

About The Authors   226

INTRODUCTION

THE SIGNIFICANT DIFFERENCE

*"I have often thought morality may perhaps
consist solely in the courage of making a choice"*
- Leon Blum

What does it mean to make wise choices? What does it mean to live your life by design? While your answers depend on what is most important to you, this much is certain: When you live your life by design, you know that you have a say over how it turns out. You act on that knowledge as if your life depends on it, and you experience the fulfillment that only purposeful attitudes, intentional behavior, and meaningful experience provide.

Yet you are faced with two difficulties at the outset. First, massive amounts of information and tremendous opportunities are pouring into your life through more channels than ever. Sorting through the noise for meaningful signals is a huge challenge. Some kind of filter is needed to weed out the extraneous and help you focus on ideas and information of greatest importance to you.   Second, life in a rapidly changing world is filled with numerous variables outside of your control, and there is always the chance that you'll be faced with an undesirable circumstance.   When life deals you a weak hand, regardless of your opinions about it, you still have to play the hand you were dealt.

These two challenges force you to contend with a basic question: How is it possible to design your life amidst so much information, uncertainty and change?   We believe that a life by design begins with the recognition that there is a significant difference between what is and is not your choice.

This book is an inevitable extension of our backgrounds and training as licensed naturopathic physicians. A naturopathic doctor (N.D.) attends a four year post-graduate medical school following standard premedical education, and receives the same basic science, clinical and diagnostic training as an M.D. . The significant difference between an M.D. and an N.D. is that naturopathic physicians focus on treating the whole patient, preventing illness and restoring health rather than merely treating the symptoms of illness with drugs and the removal of troublesome body parts. In other words, an N.D. looks at the whole person rather than this symptom or that organ. While this idea is just beginning to catch on in the conventional medical community, it the at the core of naturopathic medicine. This was brought home clearly to us in our very first class in naturopathic medical school.

THIS DOCTOR COMES IN...

*The art of medicine consists of amusing the patient
while nature cures the disease.*
- Voltaire

Our professor shuffled into the classroom and took his place in the front of the room. He had a rumpled, intellectual quality to him, as he stood there in his tweed jacket waiting for the excited new students to quiet down.

"We are going to begin your education with a two step natural treatment for body lice that works great on small children. Step one: Drench the child in 100 proof pure, natural alcohol. Step two: Roll the child in pure, natural sand."

He stood there silently a moment, his eyes scanning ours as we stared at him with questioning looks. " The theory behind this treatment is that the lice will get drunk, throw rocks at each other and fall off."

Most of the students got the joke and laughed. Many of us relaxed. Some thought that perhaps they had been mistaken in their choice of careers, and tried to remember where they had parked their cars. But we'll never forget what he did next.

THE TWO KINDS OF DIS-EASE

There's nothing wrong with you that
an expensive operation can't prolong.
- Graham Chapman

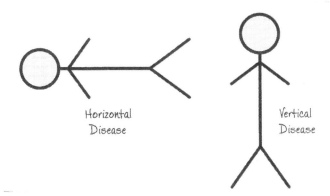

Horizontal
Disease

Vertical
Disease

He drew two stick figures on the board. There are two kinds of dis-ease in this world, horizontal and vertical. Horizontal disease is any condition or illness that lays you out flat, that forces you to stop your normal activity and change your behavior. Horizontal disease can be anything from a bad flu to such life threatening conditions as stroke and heart attack. One positive aspect of horizontal disease is that it gets your attention. If you have any sense at all, horizontal disease motivates you to take some kind of action to deal with it and hopefully recover from it.

Vertical disease can actually be worse than horizontal disease, because a person can adapt to vertical disease and continue to function in society while the quality of life is slowly destroyed. Vague complaints are often a sign of vertical disease, like when a patient knows that something is wrong, but lab tests come back as borderline 'normal.'

The chronic degenerative illnesses that plague modern society, like arthritis, cancer and hypertension, also fall into this category, as does the generally slow loss of function that people equate with aging. Most disease is vertical before it becomes horizontal.

No matter how much vertical disease a person is experiencing, the effects caused by it can be ameliorated if the person makes wise choices about what they take in, what they put out, and what they surround themselves with. Yet many people have trouble with this, because they either (1) don't know that they have a choice, (2) don't care that they have a choice, or (3) don't have the support they think they need to make the choices that lead to the changes they desire. So the default choice for the vertically ill is to accept their 'fate' as the walking wounded . Our essential therapeutic goal is to help patients learn to make wise choices in order to optimize their health and maximize their chance for a high quality of life.

People do have choices, choices have consequences, and the sum total of those consequences equals the quality of life, health and well being a person experiences .

TRIANGLE OF CHOICES

*Lord grant me the courage to change the things I
can, the serenity to accept the things I cannot change,
and the wisdom to know the difference.*
- St. Francis's prayer

To optimize the quality of your life, consider the Triangle of
Choices.

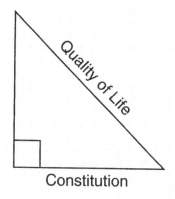

We begin with a simple right triangle. The hypotenuse of the
triangle represents the quality of your life. The longer that line, the
higher the quality of life that you experience.   How do you make the
hypotenuse of this triangle longer? You increase the length of either
of the other two sides.

The base of the triangle is fixed at birth. It represents your constitution, your genetic inheritance, or the hand you've been dealt in the
game of life.

We all have our genetic strengths and weaknesses. Eyesight is an
obvious example, but this is also true of hearts, kidneys, hormone levels and immune system response.   And your constitutional strength
isn't just a physical phenomenon. If you have more than one child,

or grew up with at least one brother or sister, you have probably observed that different children come into the world with different psyches, talents, needs and demands. You can even see this difference during the birth process. Some babies come out shouting "Here I am!" and others come out with a meek "Is this the right address?" In fact, some people are born with so much physical and psychological strength that life barely makes a dent in them. George Burns was certainly an example of constitutional strength. He lived to be 100 years old, and right up to the end of his life he was active , he was alert ...and he smoked 18 cigars a day. When he was asked, "What do your doctors say about that?" He replied, "They say nothing. They're all dead."

Such constitutional fortitude is the reason why some people don't have to put much attention into how they take care of themselves. They can smoke, drink and lose sleep and it doesn't seem to matter, they seem to have remarkable stamina that allows them to stay healthy. That's also why some people have to put an incredible amount of time, energy and money into how they take care of themselves. They must watch what they eat, what they drink, and make sure they get enough sleep, or they feel run down and vulnerable to getting sick. This accounts for the biochemical individuality that makes direct comparisons of your behavior to the behavior of others inaccurate, and reveals the value of recognizing your own individual needs. Your constitutional baseline is fixed and, while you can shorten this line through accidents and other damaging events, you cannot lengthen the base of your triangle.

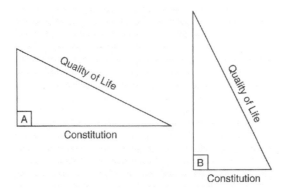

Both person A and person B represent the same degree of health, however person A doesn't have to do much to maintain it , while person B has to work much harder at it.

However, your constitution isn't just physical or psychological. Some people are born into fortunate circumstances, while others seem to have been born under a bad sign. The child of a prosperous family may gain certain advantages not available to the one born on the 'wrong' side of town, and the person born in a free society may have certain advantages over the person born into a minority race or religion in an oppressive society. And if you extrapolate the triangle of choice out to other systems, like families and businesses, then you see that each of these systems also starts out with a given hand consisting of foundational strengths and weaknesses over which members have little choice so long as they're in that system. Most people don't have much choice about who their parents are. You may not have a choice over the changes happening in the industry in which you work right now.

Regardless of what you want to achieve in life, there will likely be some factors that are beyond your choice. Like it or not, when it comes to the hand you've been dealt in life, you've got to play it. The good news is that there will always be factors about which you do have a choice, factors that you can change and factors that you can influence. These choice factors are represented by the third line, the height of the triangle.

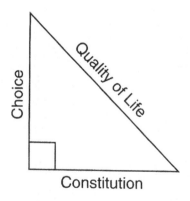

One choice factor is nourishment. In the late 1980's, then-surgeon general Everett C. Koop found that the U.S. was spending 28% of the entire health care budget on nutritionally preventable disease. What you eat, when you eat, and how you eat will all effect your health and well being. Another choice factor relates to your activity level. While not all kinds of exercise are right for everyone, some kind of exercise is right for you. Numerous studies have shown that people who exercise regularly tend to have more physical and mental energy, and are less likely to experience depression than their sedentary counterparts. Environment, from the quality of the air you breath and the water you drink to whether you live in a noisy urban or sleepy rural setting, is another factor that can influence your health and well being.

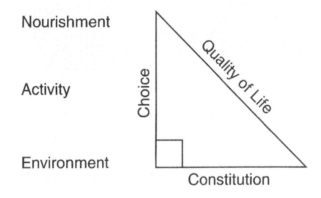

However there is more to you than food, exercise and environment. Your attitude towards life will also have an effect on your overall health and well being. For example, if you treasure life and see yourself as valuable, you're more likely to nourish yourself than if you take life for granted and have low self esteem. If you have a sense of control over your life by clearly defining your values and goals, you are more likely to engage in activities that fulfill you. And if you surround yourself with people that care about you and support you, that atmosphere is more conducive to well being than one polluted by fear, negativity and disappointment. It is a simple equation: The more of these choice factors that you can optimize, the more happiness and fulfillment you will experience. The choices covered in this book are the result of our work with thousands of patients and hundreds of thousands of seminar participants. While our list is not all inclusive, it represents the key choices necessary to living a life by design.

You can choose to optimize your quality of life by paying attention to the choice factors, and focusing on what can be done and doing it. Or you can choose to focus on what can't be done, and focus on the circumstances over which you have no control. That choice is always yours.

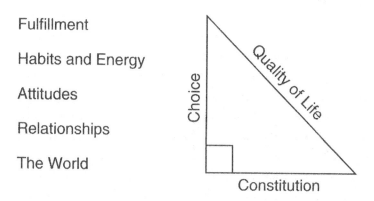

Fulfillment

Habits and Energy

Attitudes

Relationships

The World

NOW IS THE TIME TO CHOOSE

When you come to a fork in the road, take it.
- Yogi Berra

To live a life by design, you must first acknowledge that there will always be variables over which you have no choice, and variables over which you always have a choice. You can choose to experience your life as having a purpose that you are able to fulfill. You can choose to make wise choices about which habits to develop and which to eliminate. You can choose attitudes that empower you meet your challenges head on. And you can choose to make the connections that help you and support you in living a life of meaning instead of regret.

To get the most out of this book, we recommend that you start with Chapter One and work your way to the end. Along the way, each chapter has an area called 'Inventory Your Experience' that contains activities for gaining leverage from each chapter. If you do the activity and then progress to the next chapter, by the end of this book you'll have a blueprint for living your life by design in this mixed-up world. Although this book is written to be read from cover to cover, we realize that one of the four sections may have more immediate value for you than the others. For example, if you already have a high degree of clarity about what would fulfill you in life but you have difficulty creating supportive relationships, you may want to turn immediately to the 'Making The Connections' section of the book. Whether you read the book in order, or skip around according to what most interests you, we've designed the table of contents to be a quick read through, and review, of the wise choices described in each chapter.

How you read this book is your choice, and we hope you enjoy making it. Ready? Let's get started!

Part 1

CHOOSING FULFILLMENT

Fulfillment

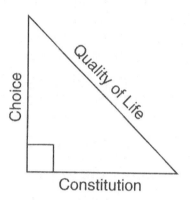

To understand the heart and mind of a person, look not at what he has already achieved, but at what he aspires to.
-Kahlil Gibran

1. MAKING A STAND

FINDING YOUR PURPOSE

Here is a test to see if your mission on earth is
finished. If you are alive, it isn't.
- Francis Bacon

Let's get right to the point. What do you regard as the purpose of your life? The end result of a stroke of lightning in the amino acid soup that somehow crawled out on land and are reading this book? A happy accident? A finished work? Something more than the sum of your parts?

If you're like most people, from time to time it occurs to you that you are here for a purpose larger than you've heretofore conceived. In those moments, you sense the vast and largely untapped reservoir of potential inside you. Some people get lucky, and find themselves doing work that speaks to their hearts and minds in a single affirmative voice. For the rest of us, purpose constitutes one of life's greatest mysteries, a grand 'aha!' that has yet to reveal itself.

Since some people do know their purpose, it must be possible to know it. And so it is. Your purpose is revealed when you pour your entire inventory of experience into your values, and aim it at the future.

Values constitute the foundation of a meaningful life. Yet the word 'values' has sadly lost some of its meaning in recent years, possibly because of preponderance of politicians proclaiming that they 'share your values,' just to name one example. At the same time, differing values represent one of the primary battlefields in many cultures around the globe. Competing camps of special interests have discovered that 'values' are a convenient wedge. Values have the power to polarize people, particularly people who aren't entirely certain what their values are, but nevertheless recognize their importance.

Many of the fundamental issues and problems of our time can be traced to a collective lack of clarity about values, and a lack of appreciation for the role they play in guiding our shared decisions, goals, plans and actions. Yet values are intensely personal, so collective clarity requires individual clarity.

OIL AND WATER DON'T MIX

A people that values its privileges above its principles soon loses both.
-Dwight D. Eisenhower

Ultimately, values cannot be decided for us and imposed on us, even by well intended elders. R. Buckminster Fuller, the architect-inventor-philosopher, discovered this while a young man filled with despair over his many seeming failures. He stood on the shores of Lake Michigan, ready to cast himself into the waters and swim until he weakened and drowned. Then he realized this was his last chance to think for himself. He became determined to use his last moments to think things through really well, this one last time.

When he looked at the competing values systems given him as a child, he realized the nature of his inner conflict. His mother had told him to 'Do unto others as you would have them do unto you,' and 'Love thy neighbor as thyself.' His uncle told him that 'it's a dog eat dog world, and you've got to look out for number one.' Suddenly it was clear. These competing sets of values were like oil and water. They simply did not mix. His confusion was caused by trying to live up to the values of those he loved most.

To end the turmoil, he had to determine for himself what he stood for and what his life would be about. Bucky was able to identify his inventory of experience and pour it into his values, aimed at the future. He conducted an experiment for the rest of his life to see what one individual, with no particular resources or advantages, could do to improve the human condition. He began living a life by design.

Sooner or later, everyone is confronted with moments of truth in which they must choose what their lives will be about. If you so choose, this can be your moment of truth, right here, right now. Taking a stand is not an easy thing to do, yet it is absolutely necessary for a purposeful life. As the waves of change swirl around you, one rushing in while another rushes out, the stand you take must be on solid ground. Your values provide a place from which you can seek your vision and achieve your goals. They provide a gauge of importance against which you can measure everything that seeks to occupy your time and energy.

WORLDS WITHIN WORLDS

Happiness is that state of consciousness which
proceeds from the achievement of one's values.
-Ayn Rand

Considering their importance, a definition of values is in order. Values are sets of personal principles by which you guide your life.

Different areas of life have their own value sets. Being a parent incorporates one set of values, for example, while the principles that govern what type of job you find fulfilling constitute another. Values play a fundamental role in successful relationships. Couples who come together and stay together have similar relationship values. But all of these value sets are subsets of the larger set by which you govern your life. For a sense of wholeness, the subsets must fit under the superset of your life values.

Yet that is not enough for a life by design. Personal values are not magic, and don't guarantee success and fulfillment in and of themselves. If your values are in conflict with the values of nature, then you will be in conflict with yourself. You are a part of nature as surely as nature is a part of you. If your values violate the laws of nature, you have no hope of true happiness nor lasting success.

Hitler, like all demagogues and dictators, had very strong values, at least in public. He valued a unified Germany. He valued racial purity. He valued the idea that the end justifies the means. But his values were in conflict with the laws of nature. His values were in conflict with the rules of human relationship. His values were opposed to the values that make the world work.

Arrogance, greed and deceit may last for a cycle or two, but no lasting future can be based on them. All of history shows that such values are ultimately doomed. If there is power in knowing your values, it is in knowing that your values are congruent within yourself, and congruent to the larger values that govern nature.

THE VALUE OF CLARIFICATION

The secret of success is constancy of purpose.
- Benjamin Disraeli

When we've asked our patients and audiences if they know what their values are, most people say yes. When we ask what their values are specifically, most of them ask us what we mean! It is a rare experience to hear someone say 'This is what I value most in life ' and then come right out and say what it is.

Whether you can readily identify them or not, values are reflected in the way you conduct your life.

While you may not be conscious of your values, you most definitely do have them, and they are observable in the way you live your life. Who you marry, how you do your job and how you raise your children are all a reflection of conscious or unconscious values. If your value sets are a mismatch, you pay the price in stress and disease. Fulfilling one set of your values at the expense of your other value sets will subtract from your energy and disrupt your ability to think clearly. It is essential that you clarify your values and bring them into alignment.

Susan, a patient with a low energy syndrome, could not get any improvement in her condition. Lab tests revealed nothing significant, and no one could put their finger on the cause of her complaint. By doing a values clarification process, she began to see a major source of her problem. Here was a person who valued honesty and integrity, who valued having her words match her deeds and her deeds match her values, yet everyday she went to work and sold something she didn't believe in to people who didn't need it. How was this possible? Because the human capacity for explanations, excuses and self-justification is virtually limitless. After all, she was an excellent sales person, and her boss showed his appreciation with bonuses and benefits. For the sake of a regular paycheck and occasional perks, she had put her survival needs into conflict with her personal values. Once she became aware of this values conflict, she was motivated to take another step towards a life by design. She got specific about the kind of career that would be fulfilling for her, and in a matter of weeks, she had a new job, and her low energy syndrome was gone.

Knowing your values is the beginning of such wisdom. Within your own value system there are values of greater and lesser importance. Getting clear on the order of importance gives perspective to the choices that you make.

Henry was a 40-something desk jockey whose weight and sedentary job exacerbated his back problem. He valued his health, and so he committed himself to get in shape and stay that way. After making up his mind to 'just do it', he joined a local health club. Every time he thought of going to work out, he would begin a mental review of all the work still needing to be done. Not going was the inevitable result. Once Henry clarified and prioritized his values, he realized that his health was a higher priority value to him than getting the work done. This clarity made it possible for Henry to change his attitude towards taking time to exercise so that he could enjoy and appreciate doing it.

Likewise, after clarifying and prioritizing her values, Laura, a mother of four children, found herself less reactive to the messes that sometimes got created by her kids. She realized how much more important a loving family was to her than having everything in perfect order in the house. This made it possible for her to refocus their attention from dealing with her negative emotional reactions to educating her children about caring for the home they all shared.

Marie was frustrated by a job from which she said she derived no pleasure. Once she clarified and prioritized her values, she was able to see clearly how her job afforded her the opportunity to fulfill her values of 'family' and 'education,' by helping her to earn the funds for her daughter's college education. Her stress level went down, and her performance at work improved dramatically. Her daughter got a benefit too, because she was released from her guilt feelings over the pain her mother had suffered to put her through college. The resulting love and gratitude served to strengthen the mother-daughter relationship.

The pattern holds true: Unfulfilled values lead to negative and counter-productive emotions. Explosive anger, chronic frustration , and quiet despair are forms of dis-ease. It would appear that we are designed to live our lives with integrity, and that failing to do so exacts a terrible penalty. You can love this or hate this, but when it comes to nature, the law is the law.

THE CURRENCY OF LIFE

If you have built castles in the air, your work need not be lost; that is where they should be. Now put the foundations under them.
- Henry David Thoreau

In a sense, every child is born into this world with some amount of 5 golden coins in the currency of life. Over the course of your life you can invest, save, spend or waste these coins as you choose. These 5 types of coins are time, money, energy, talent and opportunity. We all know someone who never has enough time because they always waste it, who never has enough money because they'd rather spend it, who never has much energy because they're saving it for something special, who squanders their talent because they figure they'll never 'make a living,' or who lets opportunity knock and waits for it to go away. One way to determine the big picture of your values is to ask yourself this question: If you had as many of these coins as you could possibly desire, all the time, money, energy, talent and opportunity in the world, in other words, if you had no excuses , what would you be doing right now? Why would you make that choice? What is it you value about doing that when you have no excuses?

Example: George says "I'd be cashing in my coins for hard cash!' Why that? "Because it would allow me to go home and have fun!" In this case, the value is FUN! Jerry says "I'd be sailing the high seas in tall ship with the breeze at my back." Why? "Because it would

28

be an adventure!" In this case, the value is ADVENTURE. Elaine says "I'd take 2 years off and do nothing!" Why that? "Because I'm exhausted." But wait a minute! We said you have all the energy in the world! What would you do if you didn't have the excuse of "I'm exhausted!"? And Elaine says "I would travel the back country of the world wearing only the finest outdoor clothes!" Why that? "Because I cherish quality clothing in the tranquility of nature." In this case, the values are QUALITY and TRANQUILITY.

If you ask yourself to answer this question every day over a period of weeks, you'll notice that the answers depend somewhat on time of day, day of the week, time of month, and mood at the time. Yet over a period of weeks, the same answers emerge over and again. In this way, your answers reveal your values to you.

INVENTORY YOUR EXPERIENCE: GOLDEN COINS

No Excuses

OK. You get the idea. Now, it's your turn. Do this now. Imagine that you have all the time, money, energy, talent and opportunity in the world! Imagine that you have absolutely no excuses to stop you from doing anything you want to do with your life. What will you do? Make a list of all the things you would choose to do right now if you had nothing stopping you at all. Then, take a second pass at this list, and write down why you would do these things above all else. What do you find valuable in them? What values of yours do you imagine these activities would fulfill?

Your Excuses

Perhaps a more challenging way to approach this is to inventory how you are using your currency of life right now! To take a stand, you need to get some solid ground beneath your feet. What are you doing with your time, money, energy, talent and opportunity at this time in your life? Why that? What are you doing with your life, and why that? What values drive your current crop of choices? While the answers to these questions may shock you, they may shed more than a little light on the trail that brought you to where you are, as well as on how you want to light the path that waits beyond the next horizon.

Values are so valuable that there's another chapter on them! So, once you've completed these activities, please join us in the next chapter and learn how to get more specific about your values in order to build a solid foundation upon which you can create your life by design.

2. STANDING STRONG

THREE SIMPLE STEPS

*You can't cross the sea merely by standing
and staring at the water.*
- Rabindranath Tagore

You can use the three simple steps that follow to develop a statement of your values. Then you can evaluate the results to see how you're doing so far in living a life by design.

Step #1: A list of words

Ask yourself what is important to you in life, what really matters more than anything else. What do you value? Consider what words come to mind. Make a list of words and write them down. Some people come up with 5 words, some with 15.

Examples from our patients and from people in our audiences tend to include words like God; spirit; family; children; health;

friendship; honesty; fun; adventure; integrity; joy; service; making a difference; money, romance.

Step #2: Define these words.

What do you really mean by the words you choose to represent what you believe to be most important in life? Define each of your words in no more than two sentences.

Patients and members of our audiences have provided us with the following examples.

Fun=seeing the humor in all situations; being willing to laugh at myself; having a good time, even when things are going badly.

Family=Building a good relationship with my children, raising them to be happy and healthy emotionally and physically.

Creativity=A life of invention, education and intelligence.

Contribution=leaving a legacy that improves the world in tangible ways.

Freedom=marching to my own drummer, measuring everything against my own common sense, exercising discernment

You may find in the process of defining your words that two of your values merge into one. For example, a person who initially lists friendship & family finds that by definition, these are both extensions of his value of love. Love might then be defined as 'Enjoying and supporting my family and friends. Taking time to be with those I care about. "

Step #3 Putting the words in order

Now look at these words and your definitions for them, and put them in order. While all of these values are important enough that they earned a spot on your list, the order of their importance is essential to your success. For example, if you have Family, Health, and Career as three of your top five values listed in that order, and then you see that you're spending all of your time working on your career, almost no time with your family and doing nothing for your health, you will instantly know the source of your inner conflict. Sort these words and definitions by order of importance now.

EVALUATING YOUR VALUES

You are today where your thoughts have brought you;
you will be tomorrow where your thoughts take you.
- James Allen

Next, evaluate your values and see whether you've been taking action and building your life on them, or have been living in conflict with them. There are four stages to this examination:

Stage One: Determine which values you are fulfilling (Getting Hits)

Stage Two: Determine which values you are only partially fulfilling (Hits and Missed)

Stage Three: Determine which values you are not fulfilling (Oops, just missed!)

Stage Four: Determine which values you are violating. (Getting Hit)

Stage One: Getting Hits

With your list of values in front of you, mentally review the past week, remembering what you've done, where you've gone and who you've seen. Each time you recall an experience that fulfilled one of these values, put a hash mark next to the values word on your list. If you've done the same activity several times in the last week, give yourself a hash mark for each time. For example, if you value health and you exercised four times last week, put four hash marks next to that value. If you value family and spent time with your children, put a hash mark next to it.

If you notice a lot of hash marks next to your values, congratulations. You have an important piece in place for living your life by design.

Stage Two: Hit And Missed

Sometimes, you fulfill your values and don't know it. In our first year of practice, we had a patient named Marilyn who told us she was dissatisfied with her progress in life. At our urging, she set a goal for herself, and we helped her develop a plan. Within two weeks, she had met her goal, and exceeded our expectations for her. We were proud of her, but she wasn't at all impressed. She was still unhappy with her progress. So we did some more work with her, she set some goals, and sure enough, she achieved them in a matter of weeks. We were impressed, but she was disappointed. She knew she could 'do better.' It was at that moment that her pattern became clear to us. She had no problem achieving what was important to her. Her problem was that she was so busy looking at where she wanted to go that she consistently failed to notice how far she had come. And since all you have in life is right here and now, the sum total of her life in any moment of now was "I hate this, I want to be somewhere else."

While in grade school, Rick and his friend Donald Leong were standing in front of the GE Pavilion at the 1964 World's Fair. To Rick, it seemed like it would take forever to get in to see the exhibit. He considered the prospect that both he and his friend would likely be in high school by the time they made it to the front of that line. Donald, unlike Rick, was cool, calm and collected, without a care in the world. And when Rick asked him how he was able to stay so calm, he said "Well, every once in a while I look back, I see where the end of the line is now, and hey, I feel better."

The lesson is simple: You can be winning and think you are losing, if you're not keeping score. It certainly is possible to rush through life, always trying to get the next place, the next goal, the next benchmark, while missing out on the pleasure of your life along the way. If, in doing this values clarification process, you notice that you are fulfilling one or more of your values, be certain to stop, look back, look around and feel good right now. Appreciate how far you've come and the progress you're making, by putting minus signs by those values you've been hitting and missing.

Stage Three: Oops, just missed!

You'll also want to consider the values you have that you have not been fulfilling. What values have you not been taking the time to take action upon? These missing values constitute a significant gap in your sense of integrity. Yet if you commit yourself to taking the time, and yes, making the time, to let these values guide you, you can fill this gap with a tremendous sense of wholeness. In fact, later on in this section of the book, you'll have the opportunity to set some specific goals and plans of action to accomplish just that. For now, put a minus sign by those values on your list that you've been consistently missing.

Stage Four: Getting Hit!

Your values evaluation also provides you with the important opportunity of observing which of your values you are violating. Why should you care about these? Values violations are a major cause of low energy, a significant contributor to a loss of self esteem, and a source of low level anxiety and depression. Because the universe in which we live has integrity, and because you are a part of that universe, your integrity or sense of wholeness is violated whenever you do something that violates your values. And since feedback is built into the system, life tends to knock you down a peg or two, every time you cross that line. You must bring yourself into alignment around your values if you want to live your life by design.

Examples of getting hit:

A person who values health, yet has a smoking habit

A person who values honesty, but is coerced into lying at work

A person who values freedom, yet is stuck in a dead end job

A person who values respect for others, yet throws temper tantrums.

A person who values family, yet doesn't spend enough quality time with them.

Clearly, these are examples that illustrate how people who violate their own values can't stand themselves, and instead become houses divided against themselves that ultimately cannot stand.

ENJOYING THE VIEW

In absence of clearly defined values, we become
strangely loyal to performing daily acts of trivia.
-Anonymous

The final part of values clarification involves keeping your values in your awareness so that you can begin to align yourself with them everyday. To stand strong while the waves of change surround you, your values provide a rock-solid reference point for all your choices, and a lighthouse of stability to guide you on your way. We'll discuss this further in our chapter on 'Holding Your Focus', but for now, here are a few suggestions:

Post Them Where You Can See Them:

Out of sight, out of mind! Post-it notes, stickies, and other visual reminders are a powerful way of keeping your values in mind. A part of your brain stem as small as your pinkie contains the majority of all the neurons in your brain. It's called the reticular activating system, and it serves as a sort of 'radar for relevance'. Ever planned a wedding, and suddenly it seemed every movie and TV show was about marriage? Ever been pregnant, and it looked like you were part of a new baby boom? Ever been interested in a new car and suddenly you saw them everywhere? Ever had a headlight go out on your old car, only to notice how many others have that problem too? Your reticular activating system is constantly scanning your environment for relevance. As soon as you clarify your values and post them in visible locations where you can't help but see them, your reticular activating system will kick in and remind you to take action, right now.

Keep A Life Log

Another simple yet powerful way to align yourself with your values is to keep a log of your actions each day, and to highlight those items that fulfill your values. Highlighting works best because items out stand out from the page. Take a sample of two work days and two days when you're not working. Write down everything that you do, as you go along, in order to make sure everything gets incorporated into your life log. At the end of the four days, open your life log, and use a blue or green highlighting pen to highlight every action you took that clearly fulfilled your values. Then take a red highlighting pen and circle the items that violate your values. This will make it much easier to weed out the red and get more and more of that blue or green highlight into the time of your life.

Create A Mission Statement:

Try putting your five words together into a meaningful sentence about the purpose of your life! When you can unite all of your values under one congruent thought, you'll have the beginnings of a personal mission statement that can shine light on the unknown path before you.

Nathan, a seventeen year old patient of ours said, "The purpose of my life is to be happy, to enjoy life, to have fun, and to contribute these things to others." Jersey, a thirty-four year old we met in one of our seminars, told us: "My purpose in life is to contribute peace, and experience love in the world." Jonathan, who is in the construction business, says the purpose of his life is 'to create comfortable and uplifting spaces where people can dream their best dreams for the future.' Karol, one of our agents, told us that her mission in life is "to be a good person and fulfill God's will for me."

Add your statement of purpose to the top of your values page, print it and post it.

FROM THE WHOLE TO THE PARTICULAR

Resolve and thou art free.
- Henry Wadsworth Longfellow

We recommend that you do some values clarification at least once a year, perhaps on your birthday, on New Year's day, or any other special day of the year that can serve as a reminder to build your life on a strong foundation rather than merely reacting to the pressures of the moment. And values clarification can be an essential part of planning for any major change in your life as well.

Once you've done a values clarification process on the big picture of your life, we're confident that you will find it so fulfilling that you'll want to do the same for more specific areas. Contemplating a career change? First clarify what's really important to you about working. What do you value in a career? Some people value working with other people, while others would rather be left alone to do their work. Some people value independence, while others value job security. And some people define security as working for a big company, while for others, security means working for themselves.

Are you hoping to find lasting love in this often fickle world? Then clarify your relationship values. It isn't enough to share a few hobbies, or like the same kinds of food. If you're wanting a successful committed relationship, then clarify your relationship values first. Once you know what they are, you can spare yourself much of the misery of the dating game, by looking and listening for the values of your potential partner before getting in too deep.   If you're already in a committed relationship, do values clarification now, because shared values are essential to healthy intimate relationships.   Do it separately, then come together and share your words and definitions with each other.   Determine what your shared values are, so that you can build on them as your relationship matures. You may find that you use different value words for the same definitions, or different definitions for the same value words.   But the values you share can inform your decisions and goals so that you live long and prosper until death do you part!

Are you planning on having a baby? Clarify your parenting values first. And if it's too late to do this first, do it now, because there is no time like the present! Whether you're a new parent, or you would like to improve your parenting skills, clarify your parenting values for your sake and for the sake of your children.   Parents who are guided by a coherent value system are likely to succeed in helping their children to do the same.

You'll notice, too, that to every thing there is a season. While your core values are unlikely to change, lesser values sets will rise or fall in priority depending over time.   For example, 'family and children' may be a high priority now, but once the kids have grown and are on their own you may find 'travel and adventure' rising up the values ladder and the 'family values' expressing themselves a little differently. While older kids may want more of your money, they generally require less of your time.   And as you age, you may find that 'health' becomes a more important value than wealth, since it is difficult to enjoy wealth without it.

INVENTORY YOUR EXPERIENCE: MISSION POSSIBLE

Take Three Simple Steps

If you haven't done so yet, start at the beginning of this chapter, and clarify your core values by coming up with the words that represent them. Then do another pass related to any particular area of your life that is in transition now (career, relationship, etc.)

1. Evaluate The Results

Now evaluate your values list to determine hits and misses.

2. Declare Your Purpose

Write a sentence that begins like this: "The purpose of my life is to live with ... " and then fill in your values.

3. Put Em' Where You Can See Em'

Decide how you will keep these values in front of you until you've deeply integrated them into your thoughts and behavior.

In the next chapter, we'll explore the process of setting your goals in alignment with your values, in order to live your life by design.

3. FACING FORWARD

HERE TO THERE

You've got to be careful if you don't know where you're going, because you just might get there!
- Yogi Berra

Once you've clarified your values and begun to see your purpose in life, you can take the next step on the path to fulfillment. Goals are that next step. Goals help you to face forward in the direction of your ambitions and aspirations. While values tend to be general, goals are specific objectives. Where values cannot not be achieved but must be lived in an ongoing way, goals are specific in their outcome, measurable in their implementation, and they have a date attached to them. The result: You know when you've achieved your goals.

Yet some people hesitate to set goals for themselves. They are concerned that putting specific goals in place will detract from the spontaneity of their lives. Others hesitate to set goals because they are afraid to fail. And still others refuse to set goals for their lives, because they don't want to interfere with the lucky circumstances that often happen in the course of our daily lives. Our goal in this chapter is to provide you with insight into the nature of goals, appreciation for the real benefits of setting them, and a process for goal setting that is both easy and fun. We are convinced that there are three excellent reasons for you to set goals:

1. Clear goals free up your time, energy and attention

2. Failure is assured unless you set goals

3. Luck is the province of those who take aim and follow through

Not all goals are created equal. Instead, goals come in different sizes and time frames.

Long and Short of It

For example, you can have long-term goals like maintaining a romantic relationship with your spouse or raising your children with both self-control and self-esteem. And you can have short-term goals like meeting a friend for lunch on Friday, having fun and getting back to work on time.

Inner and Outer

Some goals have more to do with effecting the world around you (external goals), while others have to do with developing characteristics and qualities within you (internal goals).

Examples of external goals:

'Owning a particular car.'

'Writing a book.'

'Exercising 4 times a week and weigh x pounds. .'

Examples of internal goals:

'Maintaining a positive attitude.'

'Being loving and forgiving when my spouse interrupts me.'

'Learning to appreciate my success.'

While you can set any kind of goal, internal/external, for any time period, short term/long term, this chapter focuses on helping you set life goals in order to illustrate the process.

FIVE EASY PIECES

Climb High, climb far. Your goal the sky.
Your aim the star.
-Inscription, Williams College

Brainstorm

To live a life by design, you must start with the big picture and work your way to the specifics. Begin by reading your values and then consider what you want to accomplish in life. Now hear this: All goal setting begins with a brainstorm on potential goals, which means that anything is considered possible in a brainstorm, and there are no excuses to worry about or obstacles to get in the way. You'll want to write down whatever comes to mind, and produce a large number of potential goals without filtering anything out with disqualifiers like 'there's not enough money', 'there's not enough time', or 'I lack the ability'. Certainly these things may be true in a particular moment in time. But disqualifying ideas can blind you to the real goals expressing themselves through seemingly impossible ideas.

For example, a person born in Costa Rica who is brainstorming goals may have the idea of becoming President of the United States, even though this is not an option according to U.S. law. Yet hidden behind this idea is the achievable goal of developing the power base to influence the world in a positive way. Brainstormed goal ideas are not meant to be commitments. They are simply vehicles for bringing your true goals to the surface where you can identify and then set them in place.

Categorize

Once you've completed your brainstorm, take your goal ideas and categorize them. To assist you, here are some potentially useful categories and sub-categories that many goal setting systems have in common:

Spiritual: (inner peace, study of scriptures)

Health: (diet, exercise, relaxation)

Relationships: (social, professional, intimate, family)

Career: (projects, responsibilities, titles)

Financial: (retirement, college fund, investment, standard of living)

Pleasure: (fun, travel, adventure, hobbies)   Education: (skill development, areas of interest, degrees)

See The Value

Under each category where you've listed some potential goals, write the value that each of your goal ideas fulfills. If, after doing this step, you notice that most of them don't actually fulfill the values you listed in the previous chapters, you have a problem. Whenever your goal ideas and values don't match, there are two possible solutions. Either go back and brainstorm new goal ideas based on your values, or reexamine your values based on your goal ideas.

Check For Blind Spots

The categories we've included above are meant to cover the major areas of a well-balanced life, and to help you determine if there are areas where your life is significantly out of balance. You may have come up with some categories of your own. Are there categories in which you seem to be lacking possible goals? Sometimes you can miss a category simply because it has been in your blind spot, in that you didn't realize how important it was to your overall sense of wholeness and well-being. If you find that a category is coming up empty, go back and brainstorm some goal ideas to fill it up.

Dig A Little Deeper

It is important to differentiate your real goals from ideas that represent a means to an end. Let's say that two people come up with the same goal of sailing around the world, and both believe that they will probably do this ten years from now. One of them has this idea because "Travel and adventure are in my values. I've always been fascinated by the sea. And I love sailing. I just think it would be incredible." In this case, sailing around the world is the real goal. The other person has the idea because "No phones, no meetings, no appointments, nobody. Time and space to myself. Do what I want, when I want. Go where I want." In this case, sailing around the world is just a means to an end, and the end result of independence would make a far more realistic goal which could likely be achieved sooner.

Differentiate Glimmers From Goals

Now you begin to separate the wheat from the chaff. A goal is something you're willing to take action on now. A glimmer is something that sounds good , and someday you'll be ready and willing to act on it, but not today!

Our friend Stuart wants to sail around the world. Or so he says. He plans to finish raising the family first, and there are a few career related projects in the works he wouldn't want to walk away from. That sailing adventure he dreams of seems like it would be fun, but it isn't a priority at this time. He won't take action on this for another ten years. It's just a bright and shiny idea sparkling in his mind's eye. Or is it? Just last year, Stuart realized he could move forward toward making this dream come true. He took a sailing course in San Francisco, and he talked to a financial planner about the cost of a boat. Hey, he even bought himself a Skipper's hat! For Stu, this is no glimmer. This is a goal!

Setting goals has less to do with moving forward in the future, and more to do with pointing yourself in the right direction. So, when the wind of life fills your sails, you arrive at the place where you want to be. If you fail to sort out the glimmers from the goals, you'll wind up with a goals list full of glimmers. Then every time you look at it, you'll rob yourself of precious energy because of the mistaken appearance that you're not acting on the things that matter most. When your list of values and goals accurately reflects who you are and where you want to go, you'll create the momentum and generate the energy to face forward and move ahead.

FINDING THE WILL, FINDING THE WAY

"The education of the will is the object of our existence."
- Ralph Waldo Emerson

Our friend Steve went to a naturopathic medical school because he valued health and helping other people. His classmates knew that he was a surfer from California with some ocean in his values. When he graduated, their best wishes for him included a clinic on the beach and a partner who didn't surf. Not surprisingly, he opened a practice in Hawaii.

Steve's other great love in life, music, was almost as important as health, helping and surfing. Though an excellent musician, he put that value and any related goals on the back burner in order to establish his practice. In only a few years, his practice was successful enough to fulfill some of his financial goals. But Steve's love of music and creative expression needed some attention. Instead of wishing things were different, he set some goals related to his love of music, and moved forward on them. First, he decided to bring an associate into his practice. He found the perfect person, someone happy with a percentage of the profits, who didn't want to necessarily own a clinic with all of its attendant headaches. With his practice in good hands, Steve could now take some time off and pursue his love of music, while still maintaining his income from the clinic.

For six months, he traveled, playing music with other musicians along the way. Then he attended the Berkeley School of Music in Boston. When he at long last returned to his practice, he made certain to allow time for his musical expressions. Steve had clearly committed himself to the fulfillment of his musical values and goals. Rock on, Steve!

Again and again, we find that where there is a will, there is a way. Life moves forward, and the years fly by. Clarifying your values and then setting your goals will change your life for the better, and the only real challenge is to find the will to sit down and do it.

CHARACTERISTICS OF HIGHLY EFFECTIVE GOALS

"I went to a general store. They wouldn't let me buy anything specifically."
-Steven Wright

Once you've harvested your goals from a field of glimmering dreams, you'll want to go through the list and incorporate the following characteristics in how you've written them. These characteristics are the conditions of well formed outcomes:

Be Proactive, not Reactive

It is not a goal when someone says "I don't want to feel bad. I don't want to get upset. I don't want to miss appreciating life." These are antigoals, and using them is like driving your car in reverse while you look out the windshield at what you don't want to hit. Goals must always be heading towards something, not away from something else.

State Goals In The Present

If you have a goal "I will be organized."and you walk into your office and see a big mess, you'll think, "Well, what a mess. Someday I will be organized." But, if you have a goal that says, " I am organized," You look at your desk and say, "Hey, I'm organized. I can't have this in my life," and before you know it, you're taking action on it. Stating your goals in the form of "I am" works better than "I will..." This is particularly important for internal goals, because your physiology adjusts itself to your thought.

Set A Date

Ever get married and not set a date? You would have to hope everybody in the wedding party shows up at the same time wearing the same outfits. If you're not sure what would constitute a realistic date for achieving a particular goal,then make something up. As you move towards it, you'll start to see what's realistic, and you can adjust the date accordingly. A goal must have a date attached to it. If there's no date, it's a gleam, not a goal. Some people spend more time planning a party than planning their lives. Yet if you think about planning a party in terms of the characteristics of effective goals, you'll see how simple and natural this is. "We're having a party on June 8th. Who are we going to invite?" You start writing things down, you make a list, you figure out what you have to do today and tomorrow to get ready.

TRY THIS AT HOME

Love is a canvas furnished by Nature
and embroidered by imagination.
-Voltaire

Remember to coordinate your goals and your values with your loved ones. Since you and the people you live with have such an effect on each other's lives, it is essential that you all know what each of values and strives for, so that you can offer and receive encouragement and support. If you find that there are significant differences between your goals and the goals of your immediate family members, then set the goal of finding a shared frame of reference that gives everyone a chance for fulfillment. This vital first step can end unnecessary division and produce a good result.

Noel and Teresa are a loving couple with three great kids. Whenever they vacationed, they vacationed as a family. One day, Noel was invited to go surfing off the coast of Central America with some of his old buddies, but Teresa didn't think that sounded like much fun. Meanwhile, Teresa had a standing invitation to spend some time in France with a friend. Noel had no interest in going there with her. And neither of these vacation choices sounded as appealing if they had to take care of the kids. What to do? By setting the goal of supporting each other's goals, they came up with a win-win solution. Instead of vacationing together, they would vacation separately over an eight week period. During the first three weeks, Noel was hangin' ten with his buddies while Teresa took care of the kids. Then a couple of months later Teresa took her turn and flew to France, where she spent three lovely weeks with her friend, while Noel stayed home with the kids. Dude! Tres bien! Mutual support for fulfillment is a powerful shared frame of reference. When on the face of it a family's goals seem to have little in common, sharing the goal of supporting each other's goals may help you find ways to connect the goals to each other!

Goal setting can and ought to be a family affair! Occasionally, we've heard couples express their fear of setting goals that take them in opposite directions. While it is common for the goals of couples to be diverse, it doesn't have to be a problem. Setting some goals together makes a relationship more fulfilling, while setting and achieving your own goals can bring a more fulfilled you back to the relationship. And family goal setting is good for the kids! Help them to learn about goal setting at an early age, by having each child set one simple goal. Write it out for them, and post it where they can see it clearly. Then help them take a simple step each day towards its achievement. One side effect of doing this is that by simplifying the process for a child, you quickly realize just how simple it really is for adults.

INVENTORY YOUR EXPERIENCE: HARVESTING GOALS

If you have not yet done so, here's your chance to apply the five easy pieces, plus one, of goal setting.

Five Easy Pieces

1. Brainstorm Do this now. Take some time, and allow your mind to wander freely in the realm of infinite possibilities, and see

how many ideas for potential goals you generate for activities you might engage in, skills you might learn, and relationships that you might enjoy over the course of your life.

2. Categorize Use these categories, or others that you can think of to organize your possible goals. Spiritual/Health/Relationships/Career/Financial/Pleasure/Education

3. See The Value Write down the value that each of these possible goals would fulfill

4. Dig A Little Deeper Separate real possibilities from possibilities that are merely means to an end

5. Separate Glimmers from Goals From this rich field of possibilities, now is the time to harvest those goals which you are willing to take some action on from those that are merely interesting to you at this time.

Rewrite Them

Take the resulting list of goals, and rewrite it to make sure that all your goals meet the conditions of well-formed outcomes. Make sure you write them proactively, state them in the present, and attach a date.

When you've completed these activities, please join us in the next chapter, where we'll explore the power and method of planning to fulfill your goals in your life by design.

4. CHARTING A COURSE

LIFE IS CHANGE

Our grand business is not to see what lies dimly at a distance, but to do what lies clearly at hand.
- Thomas Carlyle

The old paradigm operated on the assumption that life was objective, that it could be quantified and controlled. Yet quantum physics shows us that life is boundary-less, contains no straight lines, and consists of a complex world of interconnected patterns and relationships, ever changing, unsettling, and rich with potential. Life is an uncreated environment until you interact with it. Any plans you might make are part of the process of life and subject to change at a moment's notice, because you can't control a reality that is at its core mysterious and ever changing.

In the pools of potential that constitute the essence of reality, occasionally one can experience grace while having no plan at all! Most people have had the experience of everything just lining up perfectly, surprising them delightfully, and extracting from them squeals of excitement that they've been singled out to be uniquely blessed, and that everything is perfect in the world.

Musicians know a similar state of grace, when they get together for a jam session. They set up their instruments, someone lays down some sound, and suddenly everyone is weaving in and out of a shared field of expression, each instrument lifting the others to new heights of spontaneous creativity that somehow fit perfectly together into a seamless whole. Athletic teams experience this as well. Perfect passes, perfect plays, happening faster than the eye can see, everyone moving toward the same goal in perfect synch, weaving across the courts and fields to be in just the right place at the right time, to score the goal and win the game. In the now-you-see-it, now-you-don't unfolding of the design of life, this is how it must be. Unpredictable, rich in possibility, order out of chaos and chaos out of order.

If making plans won't guarantee success, why bother to make them? Well, musicians have sets. Athletic teams have plays. And they practice, practice, practice. Their practice is the physical expression of what planning is really all about. They physically plan what they intend to do enough times so that when they are at the point of power in this moment of now, they can act on their plan. At each moment of now, in the game or at the concert, there is no time to think about what to do, there is only time to act. And because of their plan, they can take action.

The failure to plan often means planning to fail. We've found that most goals without plans are like verbal contracts that are only as good as the paper they're not written on. Without some idea of how to proceed, you're likely to resemble the balloon that gets away before the knot is tied. It flies randomly about the room until it lands at a random spot, deflated unappreciated, and ignored. While plans do not allow us to control reality, they allow us to take action, to move forward, to bring pieces of our goals to life, and along the way, to learn that we are surrounded by resources available for our use, and advantages waiting to be taken for our benefit.

56

Now is the point of power, where the rubber meets the road. The small choices you make and the small actions you take in this moment become either your life by default or your life by design. If you have no plan, no idea of your next step, anything that demands your attention can easily distract you. But if you have defined the actions, then you can take the small steps that will ultimately lead to your fulfillment.

Organization of information and ideas is incredibly simple to achieve. So simple, in fact, that an organized person would expect everyone else to know how to do it, and is mystified by the problems of the disorganized in doing it. A person with a reputation for efficiency knows that it is pointless to try to remember everything, and so writes things down. They know it is foolish to wait and see what happens next, since God helps those who help themselves. Yet for the disorganized, getting organized feels like an almost impossible challenge. We will now demonstrate just how simple it is to make a plan that produces results. We're going to show you two different methods for producing a plan.

LOOK WHERE YOU'VE BEEN

Study the past if you would divine the future.
- Confucius

There is a time and a place for step by step thinking. In the short term, one step leads to another, and though you may step too far in one direction or the other, eventually you make progress. The closer and more available the goal, the easier it is to see the step before it. In such a case, thinking in reverse, from where you're going to where you're beginning, is an effective planning strategy. Thinking in reverse is simple. Get a piece of paper, or open a word processing document on your computer. Start at the end of your plan, the moment when you've completed your goal, and then work your way backwards.

As an example, imagine that you have the goal of owning a certain car. Move mentally to that place on the timeline where you have achieved this goal, and imagine yourself driving it off the lot. What had to have happened just before you did that? You went to the dealership. Write that down. What had to happen before that? You had to have the money. Write that down. Where would you get the money to buy a car? One possibility is a bank. Write that down. How did you get the money from the bank? You showed up and applied for a loan. Write that down. What will it take to show up and apply for a loan? You probably need some sort of financial information. If you are not sure what financial information is needed, then you probably called them and they told you. Write that down and you have your next step. That's it! Pick a day, pick a bank, and do it. This method works great with simple, external goals.

However, there is another method which works well when fulfilling a goal that seems to be more complex and challenging. Sometimes, when the goals are grand and sweep across time and space, include resources not yet available and involve people we've yet to meet, we must weave our plan of different stuff. In a quantum universe where there are no straight lines, and boxes and circles are useful fictions, the best plans and charts look like webs of relationships, weaving back and forth across a sea of possibility.

MAPPING THE TERRITORY

A thousand mile journey begins with one step.
- Lao Tzu

We're going to use the goal of 'Getting Organized,' and you're invited to follow along with the project documents related to this goal in the back of the book, or to use an outlining program on your computer.

Name The Project
First thing we'll do is give this plan a name, something that is

meaningful and motivating to consider. Since 'Getting Organized' sounds a bit mundane and even boring, we're going to call this plan 'Project Swift Eagle!'

Target A Date For Completion

Now that you know what to call the plan, you'll need to know when you want it to be completed. If you are unsure about how to determine a realistic time-frame for such a vast and unknown undertaking, make something up! A guess-timate is all that is required here. You can always change it later, because as your plan gets more specific and the uncertainty of life presents itself, you probably will!

Define the Purpose Of The Project

If you don't want your plan to be another piece of paper or computer document cluttering your life, then you've got to connect it to the important things in life. How will this project fulfill your goals and values? Rather than making a generic, uninteresting and vague description in paragraph form, describe the purpose of this plan in emotionally appealing bullets (descriptive words and short phrases) , so that the meaning is clear to you at a glance.

For our example, how would being more organized fulfill your values? Perhaps the first thing that comes to mind is: "More time, less stress." But this really says very little, and begs the questions ' More time for what? What will you do with more time? ' The answer might be "time with my family" or "time for golf" or whatever is emotionally appealing to you about 'more time.' What does "less stress" mean to you? What will there be more of? Translate a negative phrase like this into something positive and proactive. The answer might be 'more relaxation time,' or 'greater health and well being.'

Now with just a glance at your 'Project Swift Eagle' you can know why it deserves your attention.

List Available Resources

This is where you write the names and numbers of people who may be able to assist you in producing the project's results. By finding and keeping such information connected to your plan up front, you reduce the amount of time spent looking for such information along the way.

Map It Out

The main part of this planning page is blank space. This is where you will make your plan in the form of a map. First, you place your actual goal in the center of the map. In this case, you write 'Get Organized' and draw a circle around it. Now you are ready to begin brainstorming possible action steps, by looking for one thing you'll need to do in order to 'Get Organized.'

Someone starting from scratch would be able to map out the information we've provided in the last few chapters. In our example, that one thing is 'Clarify Values', so you draw a line from the central

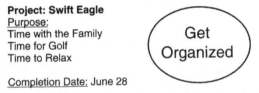

goal off to one side and write this down. You then make a line from 'Clarify Values' and write "do values process". A goals session would be another line off of the "clarify priorities line".

Perhaps another thing you need to do is 'Reduce clutter,' so you

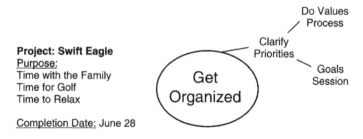

write this down. Then, map out where that clutter needs to be reduced, by drawing lines from this to 'closets' and 'desk,' and ' garage,' Now, what kind of clutter is on the desk? Paper! So you draw a line, write the word 'paper'. What can you do about paper? The answer depends on whether you have a filing system or a piling system. If it is a piling system, then you probably need to learn about filing. So you draw a line off from the word 'paper' and write down 'Learn about filing'.

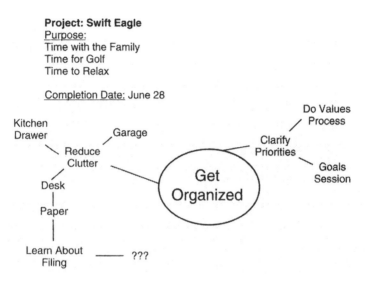

This brings you to the realization that you don't know where to learn about filing, or else your desk wouldn't look like that! Anytime you don't know what the next step is, your next step is always to 'find out'. This is one of the major stumbling blocks for disorganized people, who think they must either know what to do or they can't make a plan! They don't know that 'finding out' is a step! And what does 'Find out!' mean? It means asking someone who knows, going to the library or bookstore to read about it, searching the internet, or getting some training.

Planning is like driving in a fog. You can only see a short distance in front of you, which means you have to go slowly at first. Every time you move forward, more of the road is revealed. At some point the fog clears, and you can speed up. All plans, from changing a career to breaking a habit, to writing a book, to raising your children with self-esteem, are made up of such small steps. Though you may not know all the steps right now, it is essential that you write down what you do know and begin to move forward. Let it be ok, to not know.

Draw a line from 'learn to file' that leads to the words 'find out'. But how will you find out? A quick brainstorm produces a few possibilities, which you link to 'find out' with lines. After you 'Go to library' or 'Go to bookstore' or 'attend seminar' or 'talk to Jane' (whose desk is always so organized!) more steps will become clear to you.

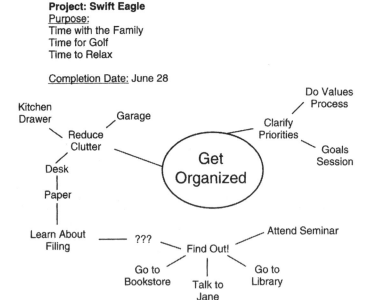

At some point in this project, the fog will lift and you'll clearly see the way to move forward unimpeded.

Let One Thing Lead To Another

Once you've made your map, look at all these little action steps and start putting them in order. You can flip over the project planning page and start making a list, or if you're using a computer you can drag or cut and paste them until you get an order that makes sense to you. In short order, you'll have an action plan of simple steps that flow in order. Mapping things out specifically is one of the best ways to get past procrastination, a topic that we plan to cover. . . later.

PLAN WHAT MATTERS MOST

"Would you tell me, please, which way I ought to go from here?" "That depends a good deal on where you want to get to," said the Cat. -Lewis Carrol

If you've stayed with us this far, you might be asking yourself what deserves this level of planning? With everything going on in your life, are you supposed to do this with everything? Obviously, if you did this kind of process on every 'To Do', every project, and every goal that you have, you would spend your life designing your plans rather than designing your life. So how do you know which goals and projects deserve this level of attention? The answer depends on your own motivations for taking action.

Every goal and every step in every plan has a degree of urgency and a degree of importance. While urgency relates to time pressures, importance relates to values. Some items are both urgent and important. Some items are urgent but not all that important. Some are important but not urgent, and some are not urgent, nor are they important. The important thing is to determine the important things, or you wind up spending your time on urgent things, even when they're not all that important.

The Cost of Urgency

When making plans, the default choice of most people is to respond to urgent items first! These people actually think they work well under pressure, when the truth is more likely that they just can't get themselves to work without it! Responding to urgency is not a free ride, because it drives up your stress, drives down your efficiency

63

and decreases the quality of what you're doing. Increased stress may lead to health problems, and lowered efficiency wastes valuable time that could be devoted to more important matters.

Non Urgent and Not Important

Non urgent and less important items tend to be time wasters that take us away from those activities that fulfill our most cherished values. On the other hand, sometimes these seemingly unimportant non-urgent activities provide benefits, like watching television to relieve some stress. But you may discover that this isn't always time well spent, since watching an hour less television a day could add up to 30 twelve hour days at the end of a year. There may not be a daylight savings plan where you can put this time away, but investing your time in the important things in life is a great place to start.

Not Urgent, But Important

Some important items only become urgent after a while. Paying your taxes is important, but it is only urgent once a year. Travel to a far off place may be important to you, but it never becomes urgent unless buying the tickets next week will reduce the cost of that cruise dramatically! And there are items that aren't important now, but you know that one day they will be.

The items most often neglected in the hustle and bustle of modern life are the important items that have no time pressure attached. Spending time with your children is important but it doesn't become urgent, and then they've grown up and it's too late. Romantic time with your spouse is important, but it doesn't become urgent, and one day you realize that the love is gone. Starting your own business might be important, but it doesn't become urgent, and then you end up in a job you hate for the rest of your life. When working with our patients and clients on their life goals, we find that most of the goals they come up with fall into this category of important yet not urgent. The point? In life, importance is often more important than it is urgent.

Which brings us back to your goals. Consider how many of your goals can be described as important, but not urgent? Which of your goals deserve specific planning?

1. Turn your goals into specific plans when they are important to you with little likelihood that they will become urgent!

2. Turn your goals into specific plans when you're certain they will eventually become urgent, and you don't want them to!

3. Turn your goals into specific plans when you have been procrastinating about them.

INVENTORY YOUR EXPERIENCE: MAKE A MAP

If you haven't applied the mapping process to one of your goals from the previous chapter, please do so now. We'll be patiently waiting for you in the next chapter, to explore the important choice of holding your focus for a life by design.

5. HOLDING YOUR FOCUS

STAYING ON COURSE

Nothing in this world can take the place of persistence. Talent will not; nothing is more comon than unsuccessful men with talent.
Education will not; The world is full of educated derelicts. Persistence and determination alone are omnipotent. The slgan, "Press On" has solved, and always will solve, the problems of the human race.
- Calvin Coolidge

You've clarified your values, the principles by which you want to live. You've set goals for where you want to go in your life, and you have made plans for what needs to be done to get there. Once you know what matters most in your life, you've got to find a way to keep it in your awareness so that you'll remember to take action! In a world where the number of communication channels increases daily, you've got to find some way to break through the noise and static right here and right now. There are at least three methods for staying on course, and in this chapter we'll describe them.

Method One: Life By Design Organizer

Whether you use an electronic organizer or a day planner, you will want to divide it into the following sections:

1. Values

2. Goals

3. Projects & Plans

4. Time Perspectives

   Month At A Glance

   Week At A Glance

   Day At A Glance

   This Month

   This Week

In the back of this book, we have provided you with templates for project pages. If you use them, we suggest that you have them printed in different colors to represent the major categories in the big picture of your life, with yellow for health, green for finance, blue for career, or any other color scheme that is meaningful to you at a glance.

Time perspectives, or calendar views as they are commonly known, are essential to your effectiveness and success. Month at a glance helps you to see the big picture on big items and major deadlines. That trip to Hawaii goes on your monthly calendar. Week at a glance is important if you have a lot of appointments and meetings, because it reveals those open spaces of uncommitted time. This open space is ideal for those non-urgent yet important items that are necessary for your fulfillment. Day at a glance may work best as two pages, one for appointments and on for items you hope to do today.

You'll want to simplify all of your action items from all of your projects when putting them into the 'Time Perspectives' part of your organizer.

Once a month, go through all your projects and decide which non urgent but important items you want to move forward on during the month ahead. Write these down on your 'This Month' page.

Once a week, review your "This Month" page and decide which of those actions you will take this week. Write them on your "This week" page. Once a day, glance at the 'This Week' page and choose the items you'll move forward on today.

Consider what you are creating in this system. You start with the big picture of your life values and life goals. You break your life goals into yearly goals. You divide your yearly goals into monthly goals for this year. You divide your goals for this month into weekly goals, which you divide into daily goals. This brings you into this moment. If you take just one item from your 'This Week' section and act upon it, you are fulfilling your life goals and values. And when you take this action, you are living your life by design. (See sample in the appendix)

Method Two: Read and Review

We recommend that you read your values, goals and projects at least once a month. Go through all your projects and pick out those items you want to make sure you attend to this month. Review your 'this month" page once a week in order to plan your next week. And review your 'this week' page each day when planning your next day.

To make this a habit, attach your reading and reviewing to another activity that you're certain to do, or to a consistent time of month that is sure to come around (It's probably best to find dates other than leap years, February 29, and all the rest of the months that end in thirty one!) For example, if you consistently have a morning cup of coffee or tea, that's an ideal time to go over your "this week" page and decide which actions you will take today. The first of the month can trigger looking at your values and goals and reviewing your plans. Reviewing your major goals and values shouldn't take you longer than ten minutes A quick glance at your monthly-weekly should take only 5 minutes.

Another way to read and review is to externalize your major goals in the form of banners and signs and post them around your house and/or office. Lisa Brinkman is an artist, and art makes tremendous demands on her soul. To motivate herself, she created a banner on her computer and printed it out ten feet long, eleven inches wide. The banner colorfully proclaimed "I AM PAINTING TODAY!" This is one of the first things she sees on awakening every morning, "I AM PAINTING TODAY!" Within two weeks she doubled the amount of devoted time for her art. You can be winning and think you're losing unless you're keeping score, so she now tracks the amount of time she spends in her studio at the end of each day. A side effect is that her banner has inspired at least one house guest to return home and paint the house!

Yet another way to externalize your goals is with related colorful photographs, magazines and books. Lindea Kirschner keeps her household together, her road-warrior husband's speaking career and travel schedule on track, and still finds the time for singing with her music group and doing service projects in the community. She works hard, and dreams of rewarding herself with tropical vacations. Then she makes these vacations happen by bringing home books from the library about the next destination she wants to visit. These books are strategically placed all over the house over a period of weeks to months, until the vacation has been scheduled and planned. Every conversation is gently turned to the topic of tropical vacations, and discussions ensue about where they might go, what they might do if they were to go to such a lovely destination. Pictures from past vacations are framed and set where they cannot be missed. For one who's tired of traveling, her husband is still amazed when he finds himself in a hammock in some tropical clime each winter, wondering just when and how it happened, and why he hadn't thought of it sooner!

Method Three: Life By Design Partner

One of the smartest ways to keep your values, goals and plans in your awareness is to find yourself a Life By Design Partner. This is not optional. We are absolutely convinced that you must do this in order to live your life by design.

Your Life By Design Partner is someone with whom you can meet with once a week for about an hour. The primary focus of this meeting is on what you want to accomplish in the upcoming month and in the next week. Such a person must have a clear sense of what a Life By Design means to you, and must have the following qualifications:

1: Someone whom you trust enough to be candid and open about where you've been, where you are, and where you're headed.

2: Someone who is logistically available each week. This can be done by long distance phone call or even by email, as long as you make it a regular meeting.

3: Someone whose desire is as strong as yours to live a life by design.

We are often asked if there are any advantages to be obtained from having a spouse as your Life By Design partner. There most certainly is! One major advantage is that it makes it possible to keep your life together connected, coordinated and on track. Even other family members can join in! On your own? You may want to form a Life By Design group! We know someone who had four Life By Design partners with whom he met regularly over the course of two years. The only disadvantage to this arrangement is the logistical difficulty of getting four people together. The upside is that with four partners, even if one doesn't show up, the meeting can still take place. With only one partner, scheduling is certainly easier, but if one of you doesn't show up, it sort of ruins the whole thing!

You and your Life By Design Partner can provide each other with these helpful services. In other words, these are your responsibilities:

Partners provide meaningful support.

This may include cheerleading, as in 'You can do it!' However, support is best given in ways it is desired and can be received, and you can determine this by simply asking "What's the best way I can support you?"

Partners provide a reality check!

If your partner keeps telling you that he or she is going to do something this week, and after three weeks in a row it still hasn't been done, your responsibility is to stop talking about the future and get current. Take a look at the seeming commitment, and find out what's preventing your partner from following through. Is there something your partner is avoiding? Something your partner is afraid of? Something about which your partner hasn't been specific? Is your partner being realistic about time? Would a smaller step increase the likelihood of moving forward? A Life By Design partner can help to clarify commitments, bring them out of the dark areas of unconsciousness and isolation, and into the broad daylight of partnership to be seen for what they are.

Partners provide the gentle push.

Rick was actually shoved into hiring some people to help with his office tasks. Even though he had great resistance, his partner said "Hey, look at where you want to get in your life. You're not going to get there unless you get through this step!" Then he took the liberty of writing on Rick's 'This Month' page, "You are interviewing nine people this month!" In return, the partner got a shove into a buying a computer system that he desperately needed. In retrospect, they both could see just how necessary these actions were. Whether it's a nudge, a push, or a shove, partners help partners move forward.

Partners Provide Awareness and Appreciation.

It's easy to get caught up in focusing on the future without appreciating what you've already accomplished. It is easy to see what you haven't yet done instead of what you have done already. Partners remind partners to stop and smell the roses, and appreciate how far they've come in getting to where they want to go.

INVENTORY YOUR EXPERIENCE: DESIGN YOUR PARTNERSHIP

If you haven't done so yet, find your Life By Design partner, and schedule your first meeting. (Give this book to your partner, and ask them to read it before you meet!)

Structure your Life By Design Partnership Meeting as follows,

taking turns on each step.

1. Review The Week

Begin by talking about what you have accomplished during the current week that was on your "this week" page. Make sure you include those items which were accomplished that were not written down and presented themselves along the way.

2. Review The Changes

Identify what you had planned to do but didn't get around to doing. Be as specific as possible about what got in the way.

3. Commit Yourself

Make your commitments for what you are going to do in the following week.

At the end of each month, do this for the coming month. At the end of the year, plan a longer meeting in order to consider what you want to accomplish in the coming year. Once you begin doing this, you'll wonder how you ever did without it! But if you haven't done it yet, there's a chance that you're dealing with procrastination. If that's the case, move on to the next chapter, and we'll help you get off the fence!

6. LIGHTENING YOUR LOAD

HABIT IS YOUR DEFAULT SETTING

Morgen, morgen, nur nicht heute. Sagen alle faule Leute (Tomorrow, tomorrow, only not today. That's what lazy people say.)
- German Saying

Is this a good time to talk about procrastination? Is there something else you would rather read about? Should we wait for another chapter? No way! We can't put it off any longer. You have clarified your values, goals, and plans so you know what is important to you. You have an organizer system and a life by design partner to keep your priorities in your awareness. Now it is time to act. If you're going to live your life by design, you're going to have to get off the fence and get beyond procrastination once and for all.

Almost everyone procrastinates, and almost everyone has their reasons for procrastinating. Before we talk about how to stop procrastinating, perhaps it would be helpful to understand the reasons for procrastination.   In case you ever need one.

Too Big

When a project or goal seems too big to take on, it may seem easier to simply put it off.   Sometimes it is so big you don't know where to start and so it is easy to just get distracted by whatever yells loudest to call your attention in the here and now.   Other times each step seems so small and insignificant compared to the massive size of the project, so what's the use.

Might as well just do something else.

The Fear Of Failure

No one wants to fail, and the obvious way to avoid failure is to simply do nothing. This is a real problem because a willingness to make mistakes is the first step to learning. Wayne Gretzky, the greatest hockey player who ever lived, and who holds the record for most goals in a season and in a lifetime said, "One thing is certain, I miss every shot that I don't take."

That Yucky Unpleasantness

Sometimes unpleasantness is just a side effect of a project that is big and complicated. Other times it is a side effect of fear of failure. But some things really are unpleasant all by themselves, like firing someone, or cleaning the cat box, or making a cold call to a prospect, or talking to a parent about how they want things handled after they've passed away. Procrastination is certainly a way of avoiding unpleasantness.

Perfection Paralysis

Procrastination is sometimes the result of caring too much, wanting to do something perfectly, and seeing all that can possibly go wrong if you move too quickly. Because you know it must be done right, because you really want to do it right you'll wait for that big block of time. However big blocks of time arrive on the back of a unicorn and when was the last time you saw one?

Jack is a perfectionist, at least when it comes to reading materials. Walk into his bathroom and you'll see that he's got the L.A. Times stacked up about a foot and a half, Sporting News piled almost as deep, and a two foot pile of law journals besides. They're all neatly arranged, but you've got to wonder why he doesn't just stick them in boxes since he seems intent on saving them all. He says " Oh, no. These aren't the ones I'm saving! I already put those away. These are the ones I'm still reading." You see, Jack not only has to read all of these magazines, papers and journals before he can put them away, but he feels he must read them in order! He told us, "In the Sporting News I'm almost up to the end of last year's baseball season." We said, "Hey, Jack. For fifty bucks we'll give you a hot tip on who to bet on in the series."

So now that we have the reasons out of the way, it's time to talk about how to stop procra.....wait a second. There is one more reason that ought to be discussed here.

Pseudo-procrastination

This is the worst of them all. That's when you think you're procrastinating and you're not. Because , given the amount of time you have and your priorities in life, the subject of your procrastination is unworthy of your consideration. This seems worthy of discussion, so before we get to how to stop procrastinating, let's explore pseudoprastination in depth.

PSEUDOPROCRASTINATION

What may be done at any time will be done at no time
-Scottish Proverb

In a busy world, it is not uncommon for a busy person to unconsciously accumulate a heavy load of incomplete actions, unfulfilled goals, and decisions left unmade. You hold these unresolved items over your head. and carry them around while they drag you down and rob you of your energy. There are times when you may feel as if you've been buried under the weight of this burden, because as it grows, (and it does grow over time) the energy requirement needed to carry it along grows as well. We call this phenomenon 'pseudo-procrastination', because, as you're about to see, it isn't real (though its effects are)!

We have found that at least half of all the things people procrastinate about fall into this category! Half! Think about that. We are sure it is half of yours too. Just think how good that can feel to forget about half of them. The truth is given your real priorities and the amount of available time, it is absurd to even consider these things. What makes pseudoprocrastination so dangerous is you carry a burden that steals energy from other important things, and it is a burden you shouldn't even be carrying. It is possible to lay your burden down, once you see it for what it is. Let us tell you the 'Saga of Handy Man'.

Rick was never very handy, but that wasn't really a problem until he bought his own home. After the first few incidents of home maintenance, he figured that it was ridiculous for him to always have to call somebody to solve every problem. His goal? Become a Handy Man! The first thing he did was go to the store and spend a small fortune on all sorts of cool stuff! He even got himself an electric drill and a circular saw! He couldn't wait for something to break. Rick also has his office in his home, and a patient pointed out a problem to him one day that needed some attention. Apparently the waterfalls that appeared whenever it rained were not supposed to be there, and there were things called gutters up on his roof that were supposed to take the rain away to wherever rain goes. Rick protested, because he liked those waterfalls, and thought of them as a relaxing design feature of his home. Sometimes, on a rainy day, he would sit and watch the waterfalls falling and the trees trembling and feel at peace with the world. His patient cautioned him that his mood would certainly change when it came time to pay the roofing bill. Rick was about to accept that the gutters needed repair, when his patient said, "While you're at it, you better get rid of all that moss!" What? Rick couldn't believe his ears! He loved that moss. In fact, he was hoping to cultivate it and create a "cottage in the woods" effect. The patient explained that this soft innocent green stuff was destroying the shingles! What was a Rick to do?

First, he took advantage of the resource and asked "What specifically do I need to do?" Then he made a plan, and waited for the weekend to come around so he could take action.

Normally, the weekend was dad and daughter family time. But on this weekend, Rick stated unequivocally "This will only take a few hours!" and headed straight to the hardware store. He bought a ladder, one long enough that you could use it to rescue people from burning buildings. And it was fun up on the roof, because unclogging the gutters was like digging in the forest primeval. First he pulled out the leaves and needles. Then the gutter clogging material became a little more granular, and then it became silty. This was a real education in soil stratification and decomposition. Eight hours later, he finished the last mile of gutters, climbed off the roof and proudly surveyed his work. He looked eagerly to the skies, hoping for more rain. In the course of a day, this mild mannered doctor had been transformed into 'Handy Man!'

The next day, it rained. Rick noticed that he still had waterfalls cascading over his windows. When his patient returned for another appointment, Rick told him "I've done everything you told me to do, but look! The problem hasn't gone away!" The patient asked Rick to explain everything that he had done, step by step. "You didn't clean out the down spouts?" Rick hadn't thought of that, so the patient proceeded to enlighten him regarding the secrets of downspouts and gutter mesh. When the patient was gone, Rick was contemplating his next step regarding the roof, when he heard his daughter's voice in the distance. That's when it dawned on him. While climbing and digging and pulling and moss-tossing was important, it was very time consuming, it wasn't fun, and time with his daughter was far more important than being 'Handy Man'. And he put away his cape (raincoat.)

What can you learn from this little story? For every action you take, there is always a time cost involved. The question is not 'Can you do it?' but "Can you afford to give that amount of time to that action?' You can do everything we've talked about in this book so far, but if you find that one of your goals takes 70% of your time, the other goals will have to divide up the remaining 30%.

When we ask people what kinds of things they pseudoprocrastinate about, we hear about recipes in a drawer that they'll someday catalog, nuts and bolts and screws that they'll someday organize, piles of magazines they've been meaning to read, construction projects that they plan to start planning one day. But it's not just small stuff, alot of seemingly big stuff will fall into this category too. But once you look at where you really want to end up in life and compare it to how much time there actually is in a day or week or month or year, you will find that you'd be wiser to cancel those magazine subscriptions, and throw out some of those 'rainy-day' projects stuffed in drawers. Pseudo procrastination is not free. You know that feeling of relief you get when you finally do something that you have been putting off forever? That relief comes from laying down the unconscious burden of an unfulfilled goal. Anytime you procrastinate, you lose some of your energy. And when you pseudoprocrastinate, that energy gets stolen from those things you value most in life.

THE WAY OUT

As we say in the sewer, if you're not prepared to go all
the way,
don't put your boots on in the first place.
-Ed Norton, The Honeymooners

To recognize pseudo procrastination, take a blank sheet of paper and draw a line down the middle to create a balance sheet. On one side write all the reasons you're procrastinating on a particular goal, and on the other side write all the benefits of moving forward on it. If the reasons you are procrastinating are that you don't know what to do, or you're afraid you might fail, or you're concerned that you might experience discomfort, and on the other side the benefits will truly fulfill your values, then you're dealing with real procrastination. But, if the reasons you are procrastinating have to do with the fact that you have more highly valued items to do, that's a different story. That's the story of pseudoprocrastination, and 'The Return of Handy Man!'

Rick's house had a toilet that ran and ran. His wife wanted to call the plumber, but Rick would have nothing to do with that! "This is a job for Handy Man!" he proclaimed. But with patients to see, projects to complete, and meetings to attend, six months passed and he still hadn't gotten around to fixing it. Then came the dreaded day when the relatively unimportant became urgent. His wife said, "Hey, I'm going out shopping. Here's the number of a plumber. The toilet has got to get fixed one way or another today. You fix it, or you call the plumber. Or when I get back, I'll call the plumber." Quickly, Rick transformed himself into 'Handy Man.' Within five minutes of beginning the job, he broke the toilet. There was water everywhere! He found the number and called the plumber who, as luck would have it, could come over right away. Fifteen minutes later, the toilet was working perfectly. Rick watched the plumber perform the repair, and as he watched, he learned something valuable. He learned that, if the toilet ever broke again, Rick didn't want to fix it! He did, however, enjoy the satisfied look on his wife's face when she came home to find Handy Man had fixed it! (Well, he wasn't going to tell her.)

Had Rick known about doing a balance sheet at the time, he would have discovered that the reason he kept putting off this particular job was that he had better things to do. He would have discovered that weekends were for Dad-Daughter quality time, broken toilets were for plumbers to fix, and that the items most worthy of his attention were the items that he valued most.

INVENTORY YOUR EXPERIENCE:
TAKE A LOAD OFF

Make A 'Not Done' Balance Sheet

Take some time now to consider those chores, jobs, and goals that you never get around to. For each item, make a balance sheet, and list the reasons for not doing that item on one side, and your reasons to do it on the other side. Which items fulfill your deepest values? Which items aren't all that important, and would steal time from that which matters most in your life?

Once you've lightened your load by laying down the burden of pseudoprocrastination, join us in the next chapter to learn how to get past real procrastination.

7. GETTING OFF THE FENCE

Know the true value of time; snatch, seize, and enjoy every moment of it. No idleness; no laziness; no procrastination; never put off till tomorrow what you can do today.
- Lord Chesterfield

MAKE A VERY, VERY SPECIFIC ACTION PLAN

Now that you have eliminated the pseudoprocrastination from your life, the items remaining ought to have some relationship to your values and goals. Here are the strategies to end real procrastination once and for all.

One of our patients, Denise, had graduated with a masters in counseling. Now she was upset with herself. Here it was two years after graduation, and she still hadn't started her counseling practice. She asked us if perhaps she needed some deep therapy to resolve an unconscious block to starting a practice. We laughed at the irony, and told her what she really needed was a plan. She wrote the words 'Start A Practice' in the center of a blank piece of paper.

We asked, *"What's the first thing you've got to do?"*

She said, *"I don't know."*

"Guess."

"Well, I guess I need an office."

"Great. Where are you going to find an office?"

"In an office building."

"Good. Where will you find out about available office space?"

"Newspaper?"

"Good! Where are you going to get a newspaper?"

"7-11?"

"Great. When are you going to get a newspaper?"

"On the way home?" Fifteen minutes later, the paper was covered with steps, and now she was laughing too, as she exclaimed "I can do this!"

When she looked at the plan she had mapped it out, it was apparent to her that it was no big deal, just a bunch of steps like going to a 7-11, or picking up the phone to make a call. Every achievement, no matter how grand in scope, boils down to the most simple, mundane

84

action steps. That's why breaking tasks down into smaller tasks dissolves the reasons for procrastination. Too Big? When a task seems too big, break it down and focus only on today's action steps. Fear of failure? How are you going to fail walking into the 7-11? It seems unpleasant? Smaller steps reduce the unpleasantness. But what about the paralysis of perfectionism? If you give yourself enough time, and make the steps small enough, you can even walk into the 7-11, perfectly.

Once you have your goals mapped out as plans, you are well on your way, with some peace of mind as a side effect. You can't swallow a whole apple all at once, but you can eat one a bite at a time.

Here are some more methods for moving through procrastination.

Schedule it first.

This is particularly effective with unpleasant items. Mark Twain once said, "If you have two frogs to eat, eat the big frog first." With the larger items out of the way, you gain some momentum for the smaller ones. And as a bonus, the rest of the day you'll feel great, instead of wasting another day procrastinating.

Do it for 10 minutes.

Make a deal with yourself that you will only do an item for ten minutes, then decide if it is still as horrible as you feared. And if it is, give yourself permission to quit. After ten minutes, the inertia is overcome and you're on your merry way! Just getting started focuses you forward on what needs to be done, and before you know it, you're on a roll and it's all downhill from there. So break it down into small steps and decide you will JUST do one today.

Find A Model

Can you think of someone who would have no trouble breaking through on a task that you've been procrastinating on? A superhero,

or a movie star, or someone you actually know? It makes no difference. First, close your eyes and run a mental movie in which you
see them doing the task. Then step inside of that movie, and find
out what it would be like to be your model dealing with your task,
knowing what they know, feeling what they feel that enables them to
move forward where you've been holding back. Now open your eyes,
pretend to be that person, and just do it.

Impose A Deadline

What gets urgent gets done. So impose a deadline and turn something important into something urgent. The deadline can be arbi-
trary, as no deeper meaning is required. That's what helped Handy-
man tackle the toilet! When you set a deadline, you add just enough
urgency to help you achieve lift-off.

Reward yourself.

Our friend Sally was addicted to the computer game Tetris.
This was causing her a great deal of difficulty while studying for her
acupuncture board exams.   But Sally used her game addiction as a
reward, and turned this time liability into a productivity enhance-
ment. For every hour of study completed, she gave herself one game
of Tetris. The studying got done, and the more focused time playing
Tetris raised her score as well!

On a three week trip to Britain with her family, grade school
student Carle Brinkman procrastinated on doing the math homework
assigned to her before leaving. With only a week left to go, and two
weeks worth of homework remaining, Carle asked her parents for
Pez! She requested that they buy her a Pez dispenser and lots of packs
of Pez candy. Then she sat down to do her homework, giving herself
one Pez for every completed math problem. The result? She finished
all three weeks of math homework in one hyperactive afternoon.

Commit To Someone

When you make a public commitment, you agree to be held

accountable for it. When you ask someone you know to hold you accountable for your commitment, you empower them to keep your feet to the fire until your promise is kept. When you keep this in the spotlight, your Life By Design partner becomes an invaluable part of your following through. Your partner can help you sort the pseudo-from the real, and encourage you to apply the strategies we've provid-ed to help you break through procrastination. And when you apply all these strategies to one procrastination item... break it down, do it first, do it for ten minutes, imagine your model, impose a deadline, reward yourself, and commit to your partner...nothing can withstand the resulting determination.

INVENTORY YOUR EXPERIENCE:

KNOW WHERE THE TIME GOES

Now it's time to get off the fence, with the following activities.

Make A Time Log

Where does all the time go? Whenever you say "Yes" to one thing in a moment of now, you say "No" to something else. It is a lot easier to know what to say "no" to when you know what you want to say "yes" to and have a realistic sense of your time. For one week, make a time log, and write down everything you do, and the time it takes you to do it. Do this as you go along, because the subjective nature of life (the speeding up and slowing down of life relative to your enjoyment) makes it unwise to rely on your perception of time for realistic time frames. Time flies when you're having fun, and anything you hate can seem to drag on forever.

Take a blank sheet of paper and start when you wake up. Write down each change of activity. If you arrive at work at 8 a.m., write that down. If you get a cup of coffee, write it down, along with the amount of time it takes. Be as specific as you can. If getting coffee takes thirty minutes, write down all the activities that led to that result. If you work on something without interruption for an hour or so, you'll only need one entry in your time log for that time. But if, at 9:21a.m. someone walks into your office and starts talking to you, that's the next moment you pick up your time log and make a notation of the person's name and the amount of time spent talking. If they ask what you're doing, explain to them "I'm keeping a log of my time. I want to see where it is being wasted." An interesting side effect of this is that it may cut your interruptions in half!

Do this at home! Keep your time log into the evenings to see where the time goes. Log a weekend, to gain insight into the way you've been using your time. For the sake of an accurate idea of time spent, you'll want to collect this information for at least three of each type of day (three weekends, three Tuesday nights, three days at work, etc.) Once you have your data logged, it's time to do an analysis.

Analyze Your Time Log

1. What items shouldn't you be doing? When you have clarified your values, goals, and plans, these items become glaringly obvious.

2. What items take more time than they deserve? In this area you may find your level of acceptable perfection is turned up too high. You may also find inefficient systems that need tuning up.

3. What 'need to be done' items could be done by someone else?

Consider the cost effectiveness of delegating certain kinds of activity to someone else.

4. How long do the items actually take? This is an essential element of your analysis, because knowing how long something takes will help you to learn to schedule your time realistically. Accurate time frames will show you how absurd those pseudoprocrastination items really are.

5. Which items fulfill your values? (highlight them) Take a highlighter and mark all those action steps that fulfill your values. Stop and feel good as they glow with acknowledgment. And while you are looking at them, notice if there are other action steps you can take to fulfill your values more often?

6. Which items violate your values? (mark them in red) Mark in red those actions that violate your values. These items can be a major source of frustration, depression, anger, low energy, and even physical symptoms. Target these areas for change by making goals and plans, and apply the techniques from our chapter about using your mind on purpose.

Every time you say yes to a lower priority item, you are saying no to those choices that truly matter. A time log makes obvious your cost in time vs. the benefit you receive from getting an item done. When you've counted the cost, you can see your way clear to saying NO to items of lesser importance, and YES to what really counts.

Once you've started your time log, join us in the next chapter to explore your ability to change your habits for a life by design.

Part 2

Part 2

CHOICES ABOUT HABITS AND ENERGY

Habits and Energy

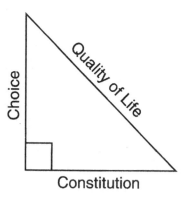

*Cultivate only the habits that you
are willing should master you.*
- Elbert Hubbard

8. CHANGING YOUR HABITS

CREATURES OF HABIT

Habit converts luxurious enjoyments into dull and daily necessities. -Aldous Huxley

Holding your focus, facing forward and moving ahead is difficult if your habitual behaviors have become obstacles to living your life by design. When we first began our practice, we couldn't help but notice how some of our patients readily and naturally did things for their own self benefit. They would aim their lives, change their diet, maintain an exercise program, learn new habits, acquire new skills, and sustain these changes faithfully! Other patients did little to nothing to take charge over their lives and improve their own health. Instead, they waited and helplessly hoped for someone (like their doctors) to rescue them from themselves, to fix what was seemingly broken in their lives. We set out to understand this interesting difference.

We found consistently that certain mental patterns produce certain results, and that both self-defeating behavior and self-fulfilling behavior seem to operate on the same consistent principles. We saw this as an indicator of basic human resourcefulness, in that the same patterns that consistently produce negative behaviors could be redirected into producing worthwhile results. If you first understand what specifically goes on when you successfully change your mind, you can choose to use your mind on purpose to change your habitual way of thinking and acting and produce the results you want in your life. Just as your thoughts and attitudes effect your health and your energy level, they can give you the strength to move past your fears and toward your goals in a fulfilling way.

You can use your brain for a change of mind, and thus change your behavior. If you have lost the manual to your mind, or worse yet, lost your mind, this chapter will provide access to your built-in brain technology for changing habits of thought and habits of action.

SPOTLIGHT OF AWARENESS

Our life is composed greatly from dreams, from the unconscious, and they must be brought into connection with action.
- Anais Nin

Your conscious mind works as a sort of spotlight of awareness, highlighting some aspects of your experience, while ignoring others. What you pay attention to and how you respond is determined by what matters most to you in a given situation. This spotlight searches for relevance, and then highlights about seven (plus or minus 2) bits of evidence to support your most cherished beliefs and assumptions. But all that other information doesn't just drop away. Instead, it is collected, sorted and managed in your unconscious mind by your subconscious mind, so that you can follow through on your conscious thought. For example, if you want to move your arm, you don't have to tell your muscles, "All right, deltoids, contract. Levator scapulae, do your thing." Like learning to ride a bike, you can know what you want to do and then learn to it, but you'll never know exactly how you learned to do it. Don't let these terms throw you. They're simply a useful description to help you get a handle on how your thought influences your actions. The point is, most of the necessary refinements that lead to action are made below the threshold of your conscious awareness.

This mechanism is in place, right now. As soon as you choose to live a life by design, you begin to organize yourself at an subconscious level to do so. It is as if your subconscious mind says "Okay, Boss, whatever you want!," Beginning in the moment that you make a committed choice, your subconscious mind serves everything up to your conscious mind that needs to be dealt with in order to turn your choice into a reality. Have you ever worried about something that hadn't happened, as if you were certain that it would? And then it never happened? This shows that you don't need something to happen in order for it to effect you. Just thinking that an event will happen is enough to change your blood pressure, body temperature, your muscles and the lining of your stomach. Studies in psycho-neuro-immunology show that if your thoughts are uplifting ones, your immune system is strengthened. If your thoughts are negative, your immune system is weakened. You can shout "Scotty, I need more power to the shields!" but Scotty must reply "I can no' give you more power, Captain! You're gonna have to start thinkin' more positive!"

GENERALLY SPEAKING

To generalize is to be an idiot.
- William Blake, Annotations

Under challenging circumstances, the problem with your mental system is that it runs on very little conscious information. Somehow, you must reduce the full flow of sensory data that might otherwise be overwhelming into seven bits of conscious awareness. You do this is by generalizing based on similarity and deleting all the counter-examples. For example, early in life you may have discovered the wonders of the rocking chair. You may not have known its name at the time, but you quickly learned that it could give you a fun ride! But, if you rocked too hard, you fell over backwards. As soon as the tears were wiped from your eyes, you formed a generalization, something along the lines of "thou shalt not rock too far back in a rocking chair, it could be dangerous."

Maybe it takes more than one fall before the generalization gets made, but eventually you learn something about rocking chairs. What if somebody made a generalization that rocking chairs were dangerous? Then, they would probably never sit in a rocking chair again, without realizing why they prefer stationary chairs. What if somebody made the generalization that chairs are dangerous--all chairs? Well, they'd find it difficult to enter any room anywhere without having a panic attack! "Ahhh! Chairs! Get them away from me!!!" Now, we're obviously stretching to make a point. Nobody has a phobia of chairs. But people have phobias of all sorts of things like dogs, the dark, elevators, relationships, heights, water , and authority figures!

Generalizations harden over time into unconscious beliefs upon which you base the behaviors that effect your health and well being. Deuter believes that nobody likes him. He walks into a room of three people, and two of the people look up and smile. Because of his unconscious belief, Deuter will delete the two who smile, notice the one that doesn't look up, and see the third one as proof of her original thought. If Enrique is the only person is in the room and is friendly and helpful, Deuter will not be able to delete the fact that Enrique is there, but will dismiss the counter-example by thinking "They're just saying that. Nobody likes me." And Deuter gets to be right, because in his world, nobody likes him. Since your mind organizes itself to look for proof and be right about whatever you decide, being right in life is the booby prize. And you can be right about anything. The question is, do your generalizations support your life by design?

When you're right, are you right about things that truly matter?

USING YOUR BRAIN FOR A CHANGE

Human beings, by changing the inner attitudes of their minds, can change the outer aspects of their lives.
- William James

While people can behave hypocritically, or disguise their true thoughts behind a smile or thin veneer of sociability, the behavioral choices you make regarding yourself are consistent with your beliefs about yourself. The person who has decided they are not athletic will avoid sports. They may never find a sport they like, and will probably be out of shape as a result. Then, if they actually do try a sport, their lack of conditioning may cause them problems, their coordination will suffer, and sooner or later they're likely to walk away from it affirmed in their conviction that "I'm no good at sports." The person who thinks they're no good at math will tense up whenever called upon to work with figures. Instead of concentrating on the problems at hand, their tension will distract them, they'll get inadequate solutions, and ultimately affirm their belief that they're no good at math.

Your health and energy are effected by your beliefs. The placebo effect is a good example of this. Technically speaking, a placebo is inert, something that produces no real physiologic response. However, it has been noted as far back as Hippocrates and Gaelin that the placebo effect is a useful therapeutic addition to medical care. In 1981, the New England Journal of Medicine reported on a study in which 170 patients with peptic ulcers were given a placebo; 92% showed improvement in their conditions. In another study, one group of patients was given a placebo by physicians and assured that it was an effective drug that would help them improve. A second group received the placebo from nurses who cautioned that it was experimental, and its effectiveness was unknown. In the first group, 70% of the patients had an improvement in their condition, while there was only a 25% improvement amongst patients in the second group. Other studies have shown that patients perceive larger pills as having a stronger effect than smaller pills, that yellow and red pills are more likely to stimulate while green and blue pills are more likely to calm and sedate. Still other studies show that patients improve faster when their doctor has a good bedside manner than if the doctor is cold and impersonal. The point here is that the power of your mind gives you tremendous leverage to effect your health, your energy, and your trajectory in life.

A depressed patient went through two years of psychoanalysis, at the end of which the analysis was 'You're depressed. Take this pill.' When the medication didn't make him feel any better, he became even more depressed, and began to spiral down into a pit of despair. When questioned, he described his past as filled with failure, his present consisting of a dead end job and a family life filled with fail-ures as a husband and father because of his depression. Asked what he saw in his future, he replied "More of the same." Depressing, isn't it? Yet when this same patient clarified his values, and began to believe that his future could be different than his past, he was able to define a direction and set some goals for himself based on his vision and values. Not surprisingly, he started to feel better. After three months, he quit his dead-end job, started his own business, weaned himself from the medication, and his depression was history. The conclusion is inescapable: Behavior is consistent with beliefs, and experience always provides evidence that those beliefs are right.

Though generalizations harden into beliefs, your mind is re-markably flexible and adaptive. This makes it possible for you to perceive an inner world and an outer world, and to keep them sepa-rate or bring them together as you see fit in any particular moment. Through nothing more than the power of your thought, you create the people in your life in your own image. Through the power of your thought, you can transport yourself through time and space, put old ideas together in new ways, make time go fast or slow without time changing at all, limit your learning to a few years of experience, or draw on and develop yourself out of the accumulated centuries of human history. And you have the ability to change internal states at will, to make a new start whenever you want.

We've found that using the resources that we possess is often merely a matter of detailing them, stabilizing and then applying them. You don't need to know everything about electricity to be able to use it, and the same is true about the workings of you mind. But when you think of your mind as an instrument that produces results, not according to fact, but according to your thought, learning the principles of changing your thoughts is an idea whose time has come!

MAKING ASSOCIATIONS

The way I see it, if you want the rainbow,
you gotta put up with the rain.
- Dolly Parton

Your mind is always making connections, forming associations between people, places and things. Some are quick and accidental. You're leaving the house and you stop at the refrigerator for a snack on the way out, and as you stand in the open door you suddenly remember "My keys are in the bedroom. I'd better go get them. But when you get to the bedroom, your mind is blank. "What did I come in here for?" But, you know what to do. You go back to the kitchen, open the refrigerator door, and the light goes on in your mind. "Oh yeah! My keys!"

Repetition and intensity make these associations permanent. You smell baking bread and you're suddenly transported back through time. That song that played over and over the first time you fell in love or when your heart was first broken gets permanently associated to that time of your life. An intense experience in a car, and getting in a car may be thrilling or uncomfortable for years. Minds will be minds, and they're always making associations.

But you don't have to be the victim of random associations. You can use your mind on purpose to break associations with the past that no longer support you (disassociation), and create the associations that will help you to live your life by design. We recall one of our teachers telling us many years ago that 'If you can be calm watching fish swimming in a tank, then you have what it takes to be calm giving a speech.' And it is true! If a person can describe an internal state they would like to have, then they've probably experienced it, either directly in themselves, or in their observations of others. Once you define and describe an internal state, it becomes a resource that you can associate to any situation where you would like to have it.

ACCESS YOUR RESOURCEFULNESS

What we hope ever to do with ease,
we must learn first to do with diligence.
- Samuel Johnson

Remember the world of 'pretend' where you spent so much time as a child? It was an incredible place of inner creativity and learning , and it is still available to you now! More often than not, there is a good chance that the resource attitude or behavior already exists in some other context in your life, or someone you know possesses it. And once you've identified the needed resource and located it, you've got to intensify your experience of it.

Determine what attitude will enable you to change your behavior.

This works best if you work undisturbed for ten minutes. Closing your eyes may help you to concentrate.

Frank, a securities salesman, felt like a failure whenever a client canceled an account. He wanted to be more determined in the face of failure.

Marguerite felt intimidated by her 'obnoxious boss.' When asked what resource she needed, she replied "If I could just stand up for myself, that would be great."

Locate the resource somewhere in your life

When Frank thought about where he might have the resource of determination in the face of failure, he realized he had it when he played softball. If he made an error, he didn't quit the game and walk off the field. He got more focused, and more into the game. At this step he imagined himself playing softball at one of those times when he had such determination. Then he explored the specifics of what it's like to be in that state. What does he feel when he's determined? How does he breathe when he's determined? How does he hold himself, what does he tell himself, and what tone does he take with himself when he's determined in the face of failure? How does he view the failure that allows him to feel determined? The more specific you are about how you are when you're in that resource state, the easier it will be to associate it to another situation.

Marguerite told us that she had never stood up to an obnoxious person in her life! But when asked if she knew of anyone who could handle her boss, she laughed and said "Katharine Hepburn! She'd show him a thing or two!" While Marguerite had never met the famous actress, her internal representation of Ms. Hepburn was the only resource she needed.

At this step, Marguerite imagined getting inside the experience of being Katharine Hepburn. What does Katharine feel, how does she breathe, how does she hold herself, what does she tell herself and in what tone, how does she view the world and her place in it?

When you focus on your resource like this, you are associating yourself to it. The more you concentrate on it, and the more times you repeat it, the stronger your experience of resourcefulness gets. We suggest you explore your resource three times before moving to the next step.

Associate the Resource to A Trigger

To truly make deep behavioral changes in yourself, you've got to be specific not only about what changes you want to make, but also about where and when you want these changes to occur. The context of your old behavior can then become the trigger and signal for new behaviors, attitudes, thoughts and feelings. For Frank, the trigger to feel like a failure was a client canceling an account. For Marguerite, the trigger for feeling intimidated was whenever her boss threw a temper tantrum.

This is where mental rehearsal comes in!

Frank accesses the internal state of determination playing softball while imagining a client canceling an account. And feeling that determination, he explores how he will handle that situation differently.

Marguerite recalls a time when her boss threw a temper tantrum, and imagines herself as Katharine Hepburn in that situation. Then she explores how she would handle the situation differently.

Do your Reps

Your next step happens later when you do your repetitions. The more times you repeat this mental fantasy the stronger the new association will become and the more likely you will respond in a new way the next time you are in that situation. Every time your mind tries to show you an obnoxious rerun about that situation in the past (for Frank a client canceling, for Marguerite the boss having a tantrum) immediately replay it in a resourceful way. Even if you only do this as often as you recall the difficult past, the number of repetitions will be sufficient for the new association to take root.

And sure enough, that's what happened. Frank found that the next time a client canceled, he automatically got determined and focused, instead of feeling like a failure. Marguerite found small but steady improvements in her assertiveness. She even surprised herself with a waiter in a restaurant. Her food was not what she had ordered and, without thinking, she had sent it back, something she'd never done before in her entire life. Like tossing a rock into a pond, the ripples effect all areas of your life, once you change your mind.

INVENTORY YOUR EXPERIENCE: NEW HABIT GENERATOR

Now it's your turn to use your brain for change. Identify a situation where you want to respond in a new way, or feel a new response, or see something in a new way or hear something in a new way. Then, use this handy dandy New Habit Generator:

Replace A Habit

1. Know what you want. Decide what new habitual response you want to have in a familiar situation. Be specific about what you do want to do, rather than what you don't want to do in that situation.

102

2. Pick a Resource State. Identify a context where you have this resource state, from staring at a fish in a bowl to feel calm, or dialing a familiar phone number as a way of experiencing confidence. If you can't find it in your own experience, think of someone else who has this internal state as a resource.

3. Create an association. Get specific about the way this internal state feels, the way you look at something while having it, the way you breathe, your body posture, and as many other details as possible, until you have a strong experience of the resource. What do you see, hear, feel, or think when you have this new response?

4. Connect the Resource. Associate the resource to the situation. Imagine yourself in the familiar situation with this internal state. If you're doing this right, you'll feel a little disoriented at first. Associate the resource to the signal that will trigger the change. How will you know when to do this? What will be the first thing you see, or hear, or feel that tells you it's time for the new behavior?

5. Review and Preview. Practice doing this several times using a past experience, then make up a new one and imagine having this new response the next time you need it, in the future.

Do this now, then join us in the next chapter where we'll explore the idea of review and preview in learning your lessons so that you finish old business and get on with living your life by design.

9. LEARNING YOUR LESSONS

LEARNING FROM HISTORY

After all, what is reality anyway?
Nothin' but a collective hunch.
- Jane Wagner

In the last chapter, you had the opportunity to form a new association to an old situation in order to change the way you respond to it. This change pattern takes advantage of a natural process with which you're already familiar. Anytime you have a bad experience, then mentally play it again in the same way, you increase the likelihood that the next time you're in a similar situation, you will do an even better job of having a bad reaction. Anytime you review a bad experience in a more resourceful way, you change your response to it in the future. Life keeps giving you a chance to learn new responses, until at last you seize the moment and make the most of it.

Your personal history is a continually unfolding story that offers you numerous opportunities to learn new lessons to apply as leverage to make your responses tomorrow different than yesterday's reactions. Yet the future does not just repeat the past, and that makes it difficult to prepare for every eventuality. You know how it works: Something new happens, and suddenly you're at a loss again. No matter how much you learn, no matter how determined you are to live your life by design, inevitably the unexpected occurs, and you're faced with a new challenge that requires new learning before you can get back on track. When it happens, it is always a surprise, and you're on the spot. Sometimes, it can seem like the whole world is watching.

At least that's how it seemed to Rick when he was invited to be master of ceremonies for a local melodrama. The owner of the theater was his friend, and she called him on very short notice, explaining that her M.C. had called in sick, and she needed his help for the show to go on! "What's involved? I've never done this before!" said Rick hesitantly. But the job description she gave him sounded so simple. "It's easy," she said. You teach the audience the rules about when to boo, and when to shout hooray! Then you tell a quick joke, set up the next scene, and leave the stage. You do this 20 times, once for each act. Take a bow, exit stage right! And that's it! " It sounded so easy. "I'll do it!" Rick enthusiastically replied.

But that wasn't it, and it wasn't easy. Nobody told Rick that the heroine had given twenty tickets to her relatives, that they had all gotten drunk on the way to the theater, that these twenty drunk relatives would be in the audience that night, and that their ring leader would be her father. Nobody had prepared him to wait helplessly in the wings as they teased and insulted her each time she appeared. Her father's crude behavior, while apparently quite entertaining to the other relatives, had the opposite effect on his daughter. Embarrassed practically to tears, she started dropping her lines. Perhaps because they were sympathetic to her plight, the rest of the cast was dragged down with her.

Not one to stand idle, Rick sprang into action. He walked out on stage and stopped the show. The crowd gasped, as he appealed to the drunken relatives for a little human decency. "What you're doing isn't funny," he lectured. "It's wrong. These cast members worked long hours to make this show a pleasant evening's diversion. This audience has paid to see the show, and your behavior is ruining their evening. Please, exercise a little self control. Now, let's return to our play."

His efforts were effective. The drunks changed their behavior. Now they turned their attention to Rick. Whenever he appeared on stage, they were as crude and insulting as they could be. Rick was beside himself. He had no idea how to deal with such horrible public behavior. Halfway through the show, feeling remarkably humiliated, he sputtered the words "I don't need this kind of abuse. I'm a professional!" and left the stage, got in his car and drove home, his last words to the audience ringing in his ears. Have you ever had something bad happen to you, and you played it over and over in the privacy of your own mind, so you didn't miss out on any of the badness in the experience? By the time he got home, he had successfully turned this bad experience into a nightmare.

But Rick understood the idea of resourcefulness. Heck, he'd been teaching it for years! As he sat in his car, parked in his driveway, he asked himself 'What else could I have done? What would have made things different?' Nothing came to mind. Then he thought 'Who do I know that would have known what to do with those rude people?' and instantly he thought of Gary, someone who rarely takes anything seriously, and sees the humor in most situations. Rick could recall more than one occasion where Gary had responded to public insults, giving as good as he got. And when he thought of Gary standing on stage dealing with the drunks, he could imagine the ease and grace with which this problem could have been solved. Inspired by this mental movie, all Rick needed was some good heckler material, so he got himself a book at the library, and memorized 20 rotten (*yet funny) things to say to people behaving badly in public. He imagined himself back on stage, dealing with those drunks, only this time he was armed with responses. After several such mental rehearsals, he knew he was ready to deal with this situation if it ever came up again.

106

You know when you're ready to face a situation that used to be difficult. It's called eagerness, the wanting to actually try it out and get the new result. Rick called the owner of the melodrama and asked for a second chance. She said 'But you left the stage!' After numerous apologies and a promise never again to leave the stage before the show was over, she agreed to give him one more chance, the following weekend. And when the weekend came and Rick drove to the theater, all the way there he prayed for hecklers.

He got what he asked for, and this time, he was ready. When a loud guy in the front row tried to heckle him, Rick turned to the audience, pointed at the heckler, and said, "I don't know if you can see this guy! He's wearing a plaid shirt and glasses, here in the front row. He's angry, that's why he's acting that way. And he's got good reason to be angry. Turns out he was abandoned by wolves as a child and raised by his parents!" The audience laughed. Rick fired off nineteen more insults while keeping his own sense of humor. The audience now roared with laughter. And the funny thing was, the heckler seemed to be enjoying it as much as everyone else.

As you preview doing new behaviors, you must imagine yourself doing them from the inside out, rather than seeing yourself as an observer. Look through your own eyes, as if you are there in that past experience, and feel yourself doing the new behavior. Repetition and intensity will lock this in to your nervous system and change the way you think and act. Once you're comfortable doing the new behavior in the past, project it forward into the future. Imagine a new situation where the new behavior will be useful. The more real you make the fantasy, the more likely it is that the change will take hold. Positive review, and positive preview make it possible for you to change your mind and develop options that might otherwise be unavailable to you.

Do this often. Every time your mind tries to show you an undesired rerun of the past, see it as an advantage waiting to be taken! Remember it the way you would have wanted it to be, as if you are there. You can either complain about the garden hose getting you wet, or you can grab the end and start watering the garden with it. If you get into the habit of reviewing the past and previewing the future the way you want them to be, you'll be making the kind of useful associations needed for a life by design.

PAVED WITH GOOD INTENTIONS

Sometimes the Magic Works. Sometimes it doesn't.
- Dustin Hoffman, in the movie 'Little Big Man'

There's a caveat in all this. Every once in a while, after you've used your mind on purpose in the way we just described, the trigger will get fired, the signal will get sent, and yet the resource for some reason won't become available, the new behavior won't take the place of the old one. If you know that you did an effective job at previewing the new behavior in association with the appropriate signal for change, and still nothing has changed, then the likelihood is great that your old behavior meets a need of yours that the new behavior has not addressed.

We have found it to be a useful assumption that behind every behavior is a positive intent. In our book 'Dealing With People You Can't Stand,' we explored the positive intents behind pushy, negative, wishy washy and disruptive behavior, using what we call the 'Lens of Understanding.' In each case, by ascribing a positive intent to people behaving badly, all sorts of opportunities open up to fulfill the intent and bring out the best in people at their worst. The same holds true for your dealings with your own problem behavior: To bring out the best in yourself, you must find and fulfill these positive intents before old habits of thought and action will go away .

Take the example of people who continue their habit of smoking, in spite of the evidence that smokers are increasingly looked down upon by other members of society and the habit itself is linked to all manner of horrible disease . Yet some people continue to smoke in spite of all the back pressure to change the habit. On closer investigation, one finds that before most smokers develop their addiction, they smoke because it makes them feel cool, or more grown up, or helps them fit in, or gives them a way to rebel against authority. Over time, new positive intentions may develop for existing behaviors, like giving the smoker an excuse to take a break from the action, or a way to give themselves a little reward, or a way to have some control over strong emotions, or a way to feel a small sense of accomplishment as a cigarette disappears. These secondary gains of smoking must be dealt with before many people can break the association to bad habits.

Many problem behaviors have unconscious positive intent as their motivators. For example, a patient who was struggling with her weight told us about her daily task of running errands for her husband. She didn't like running these errands for him, so she rewarded herself on every run by stopping at a mini-mart or donut shop and having a 'treat.' She didn't realize her desire for sweets was an unconscious intent to reward herself. Such patterns of unconscious intents are typical of people with habits that seem to resist change.

An overweight patient who had been abused in her childhood had somehow learned that the best way to protect herself was to gain weight, to be bigger and less attractive. In this case, protection is an unconscious positive intent. Until she found other ways to protect herself, she was unable to control her impulse to overeat.

Such unconscious positive intent can also produce attitude problems! You know that really negative person for whom nothing is right and everything is wrong? They may have learned from bitter experience to have low expectations if they want to avoid disappointment. A history of having your heart broken could lead to the development of a protective behavior, the inability to trust. A history of having your head regularly held in the toilet by the jocks in the high school gym locker room could lead to the protective behavior of having a strong aversion to working out. And if you're eating as a reward, smoking as a way of taking time out, drinking as a form of relaxation, avoiding the gym or avoiding committed relationships, these behaviors won't just go away.

Nature hates a vacuum. You can't replace something with nothing. You've got to find other ways to relax that do not involve drinking, other ways to reward yourself that do not involve eating, other ways to call time out that do not involve smoking, other ways to feel safe when you go to workout, or to feel safe in sharing yourself with another person who may one day go away.

Contrary to how it may seem, unconscious positive intents are not out to sabotage you with problem attitudes, symptoms and behaviors. When the negative person can no longer stand their own negativity, when the overweight person can no longer stand the burden, when the smoker wants desperately to be able to breathe freely again, when the out of shape watch workout equipment infomercials like they were real TV programs, when the broken hearted people yearn for lasting love, these are signs that the old attitudes and behaviors have outlived their usefulness, and that there are now better ways to attend to the positive intentions.

When your problems surface in your awareness as problems, we find it instructive and constructive to interpret them as signals from your subconscious that you're ready for a change and able to make new choices.

If your conscious mind sets the direction, then your unconscious is likely to follow. For example, if you go to marriage counseling and have a great session, you can almost expect that within the next few hours you will have a major fight with your spouse. Does that mean you failed to learn the lessons of counseling? No, it is your unconscious giving you an opportunity to apply those learnings.

STANDING AT A CROSSROADS

I'm fixing a hole where the rain gets in,
and stops my mind from wandering.
- The Beatles

We've come to see that consciously and unconsciously, people make the best choices they can, given what they have to work with at the time of their choosing. While many difficult behaviors have hidden meaning that can be dealt with in the way we've described, some behaviors are so deeply engrained and complex in structure that they are best dealt with in the presence of a trained professional or within a network of support. When you find yourself dealing with intransigent behaviors that are truly resistant to change, you would be wise to find a doctor or counselor who can work with you to surface hidden intents and creatively find other ways to fulfill them.

One thing is certain: Those who fail to learn the lessons of their personal history (or herstory) are doomed to repeat them. To let go of the past, you must learn something about yourself both in the past and in the present. Those learning can inform your present as you design your future. Frequently, we hear our patients and participants in our workshops say "If I would have known then what I know now, things would have turned out differently." Your past gives you perspective and advantages if only you will learn from it, let it go, and move on. In each moment you find yourself standing at a crossroads, faced with the fact that even in the presence of internal challenges, you always have a choice.

INVENTORY YOUR EXPERIENCE: BACK FROM THE FUTURE

Make a list of your bad habits, shortcomings, compulsions and weaknesses. Then do the following with each item on the list.

1. Recall your earliest memory. Allow yourself to reflect back on your earliest memory of engaging in the problem behavior, experiencing the compulsion or weakness. Who was there? What happened? How did you deal with that situation specifically? What did you decide about the situation? What did you decide about yourself? What did you decide to do? What did you decide never to do?

2. See your options. What do you know now that you didn't know then? How else might you have interpreted the situation? How else might you have dealt with the situation that would have produced a different result? If you had to do it over again, what would you do differently?

3. Review and Preview. Mentally review the experience, knowing then what you know now. Do this a few times, until the new version of that old memory is familiar to you. Then look forward to the next time when you're likely to deal with that habit, weakness or compul-

sion, and imagine yourself dealing with it in the new way.

When you've completed this activity, please join us in the next chapter, as we examine the challenge of complacency in an often overwhelming world, and how to shatter the chains of complacency in order to live a life by design.

10. ENERGIZING YOUR ENERGY

STATION RESEARCH LAB

Know thyself.
- from Plutarch

One of the greatest challenges of living is having the energy for it. The wear and tear of gravity, day to day difficulties, the bad behavior of others, the demands of balancing a career and a family are all factors that can place demands on your energy. Some people see themselves as machines that wind down with age. Or they think that they have only a limited supply of energy available, and that it isn't enough. They live as if what little there is must be conserved for some future moment. In fact, living your life by design instead of by default requires an abundance of energy.

At the same time, a life by design actually provides the energy that it requires! For example, the sense of wholeness that you experience when your habits match your values and your words match your deeds can be exhilarating. Charting a course and then moving forward on your goals will invigorate and excite you. As you bring more of yourself online and into action, you discover that you have untapped reservoirs of energy just waiting to be utilized. You can free up significant amounts of energy in the present by resolving negative associations that held you back and dragged you down in the past. Refusing to discharge negativity onto others or to have negativity discharged onto you can also free up a lot of energy. So can venting the exhaust when you're feeling backed up or boxed in. Regardless of your current health condition, age, job and relationship situation, you have access to more than enough energy to start living your life by design, because there are numerous ways to enhance and increase the energy available in your energy system.

Just for fun, think of your body as a space station, and your mind as a research lab in the engineering department. On the station, you have sensor systems (5 senses), defensive systems (your immune system), fuel intake and sanitation/recycling systems (digestion and respiration), and an onboard computer system (brain and nervous system). Your engineering department, through a complex inter-relationship of ingestion, digestion, circulation and biochemistry, works around the clock to produce sufficient energy for these various systems to run. Any disturbance in any of your systems can cause a decrease in the energy available to the station. Likewise, improvements in any of these systems will cause an increase in energy available to the station.

ENERGY SHIFTS

The world belongs to the energetic.
- Ralph Waldo Emerson

Every day, you expend energy and replenish energy. And every day you have the opportunity to conduct energy experiments, to learn what depletes your systems and what recharges them. By paying attention, you have access to valuable information that you can use as leverage to shape tomorrow into something different than yesterday. If, over time, you notice where you can recharge your shields and block the expenditure, then you can apply ounces of prevention instead of relying on pounds of cure. Hate waiting in lines? Go early, or turn the line into an opportunity to get some reading or work done as you stand there. Hate traffic and noise? Pick your travel times to avoid the worst of it, or reduce the number of trips you make by organizing to get many things done on the same trip. If you hate housecleaning but love listening to music, listen to music while cleaning your living space.

Mary used to drag herself to work, then drag herself home at the end of the day. She always felt like she was racing the clock, always one step behind, never quite able to catch up with herself. After observing her energy changes over a period of several weeks, Mary learned that she could shift the energy by getting to work early instead of waiting until the last minute, as had been her habit. An early arrival gave her a buffer in case of delays, and time to catch up on leftover activities from the day before. By arriving with time to spare, she could begin her day with a little peace and quiet, settle down and get organized, and even plan ahead for recharges she would need later in the day. The result of this simple energy shift is that Mary now experiences having more than enough energy and more than enough time. Sometimes she even gets a few steps ahead of herself!

William used to hate the noise and smells and lost time of waiting in traffic. Sitting in a car going nowhere was guaranteed to get him irritable and out of sorts, and his bad mood could sour his whole day. After observing his energy fluctuations over a period of weeks, William found a way to change all that. While he still has to spend time sitting in traffic, now he actually enjoys traffic jams! What made this dramatic energy shift possible? He keeps a wide variety of motivational, educational and entertainment tapes in his back seat, and plays them on those long commutes, or whenever he's stuck in traffic. Some days he plans what he's going to listen to. Other days, he just reaches back into the box, and allows himself to be pleasantly surprised with the day's program. He likens this to going to an interesting class or show every time he does this, and when he finally arrives at his destination, he feels like he's a smarter and happier person for it.

Energy shifts can make a huge difference in the overall energy available to your systems.

VENTING THE EXHAUST

80% of the people you complain to just don't care
about your problems, and the rest are happy
that it's you having the problems instead of them.
- Les Brown

Life can be filled with frustrations and disappointments which leave behind exhausted energy. This exhaust takes up valuable space, increases inertia and blocks out intention and focus. Not wanting exhausted energy to build up in the system, the smart captain finds an effective way to vent it safely! But there's a difference between pouring the exhaust into your living area and venting it where it will do no harm. Dumping the exhaust is harmful and contagious, whether you're doing it in someone else's space or they're doing it in yours. Whenever exhaust is discharged, it creates a negative feedback loop that brings it back multiplied, as other people mistake the signal as an invitation to unload their exhaust too!

While both venting the exhaust and dumping it require the participation of others, there are a few tell-tale indicators that someone is contaminating the living space instead of cleaning it up:

1. Bad feelings are discharged without first getting permission.

2. There is no stated intention of changing anything.

3. There is no personal accountability, and somebody else is to blame

4. There's no limit to how much or how often it takes place.

When you're starting to get backed up, notice it and take action to vent it quickly. The longer you wait, the harder it is to get it out of your system. Venting the exhaust requires assistance, so you'll want to be wise in choosing your assistant. If you're already backed up with your friend Nancy, she may not be your best assistant for venting. Vent the exhaust first with someone else, then you and Nancy can have a constructive exchange. Venting is a healthy choice, so you don't need someone to feel sorry for you, try to fix you, or think of you as broken somehow. Venting is based on agreements, so when you find someone to help, make certain that you do the following:

1. Get permission. "I'm getting backed up and I need to talk. When are you available?" There's a time and a place for everything, but all the time is rarely the best time to clean up exhausted energy. Make certain that your listener can give you their full attention.

2. Set a time limit. "I need about five minutes of your time." You'll want enough time to reflect on what you're saying, but not enough time to repeat it. The idea here is not to get into the exhaust, but to get through it and get rid of it.

3. Agree about the ground rules. "Is it okay to yell? Should I yell into a pillow? Can I throw things? Is breaking windows or plates acceptable?" By establishing the parameters up front, you won't have to worry about your helper taking your behavior personally.

4. Agree to have it end. "Please let me know when the five minutes are up." It is important that there be an end point to venting the exhaust, or you might exhaust yourself while venting it.

5. End with a next step. When you've vented the exhaust, then

what? A commitment to action is the way out of reaction. This closes the seal on the exhaust, and helps to replenish the positive atmosphere that has been displaced by it.

KEEPING A CAPTAIN'S LOG

The essence of knowledge is having it, to apply it;
not having it, to confess your ignorance.
- Confucius

The logic of energizing your energy is inescapable. Whenever something depletes your energy, you must make it your goal to find a way to recharge, to compensate you for the energy expenditure. Never wait to do a recharge until you're deeply buried, severely backed up, or completely exhausted. When you're down so low it looks like up, that's a good sign that you're in a bad way and you've waited too long. You'd better get back to the lab and start keeping track of the results of your energy experiments.

Keeping track is necessary, at least at first, or the data you're collecting could be lost in the crush of events. When you fail to keep track of your observations, your energy system may fill up with negative repetitions that weaken your shields and increase the danger. When you take the time to observe the fluctuations and write down your observations, your whole energy system becomes obvious to you in very little time, and is soon subject to your refinements.

INVENTORY YOUR EXPERIENCE: LAB STUDIES

Make A Recharge List

Make a top ten list of your favorite things to do. Then determine which of these activities requires other people, and which of these activities you can do when you're alone. If your top ten activities all require the participation of other people your list may be out of balance, and so is your life. It is important to include pleasurable activities that you can do on your own, and pleasurable activities that you can do everyday.

Next, determine how much time each of these ten activities requires, including travel to and from. If your top ten activities are all time intensive, your list is out of balance and so is your life. It is important to have pleasurable activities that can be done in short time blocks as well as the longer ones. A few three minute recharges a day can make a tremendous difference in your energy. Planning them ahead of time helps ensure that you will take the time for recharge and renewal.

Once you've completed these activities, join us in the next chapter to learn how to increase your power for a life by design.

11. INCREASING YOUR POWER

PEAK CONDITIONING

A bear, however hard he tries,
grows tubby without exercise.
- Pooh's Little Instruction Book

Exercise is a phenomenal power generator, which explains the correlation between sedentary living and low energy levels, and the difficulty a sedentary person experiences when they try to get up off the couch. Just as you need to provide your body with nutritional, mental and emotional fuel, you also must move it or you'll lose it as the fuel turns to fat. The energy generated by exercise can strengthen your heart , lower your risk of stroke and heart attack , oxygenate your tissues and organs, tone your muscles and skin, and help you have a body that doesn't frighten or depress you when you look in the mirror. Yet few people are motivated to exercise for these benefits alone. We've found that people who truly enjoy exercise and take the time for it are using it to energize themselves. Exercise, for those who have learned to love it, is a great way to spend time in nature, to wake up to the newness of each day, to share some time with good friends or conversation with loved one. Exercise is also a great way to meet energetic people who can support you in your life by design.

The challenge of exercise is to find the right program that address-es your concerns about how exercise might constrain you. Finding the time to exercise seems like an impossible task to someone who is already overwhelmed by work and family responsibilities. Clearly, such a person must find a way to integrate exercise with either family or work. A husband and wife can go to the gym together, or take long walks in the evening. We know one patient who used to be in shape, until his dog died. He realized that he had to start taking walks with his wife or else get a new dog. A workout machine in your home can eliminate the travel time of going to and from the gym. If you choose, you can integrate exercise into your normal activities. Wherever you go, park in the farthest corner of the parking lot, and then always take the stairs instead of elevators. Instead of meeting a client for lunch, meet for an activity. A long walk followed by a light lunch can clear your mind.

Physical limitations don't have to limit you. Where there's a will there's a way. If you have arthritic knees, swimming is a healthier form of exercise than running, and running on natural surfaces is better than running on pavement. People with structural problems affecting their backs and joints should consult their physician before starting any exercise program, and the same is true for anyone with a chronic illness. Yet one of the advantages of the changing world we live in is that there are now more choices than ever in forms of exercise, and exercise equipment has been developed to meet virtually anyone's physical needs. Ultimately, a well defined exercise program will produce the energy you need to fulfill your goals and values, so make a plan and schedule it.

To get into peak condition, sometimes you have to start from the foot of the mountain. You can't get to the top in a single bound, and any attempt to do so will only bring you up short. Instead, step by step, make your way until the view becomes so engaging, the recharge so stimulating, that exercise becomes nothing less than dynamic living at its best.

FOOD AS FUEL

"Tell me what you eat,
and I will tell you what you are."
— Anthelme Brillat-Savarin

Though there are many psycho/emotional/social reasons for eating, as far as your body is concerned, eating is a simple matter of survival. Food provides the raw materials that your body needs to re-build itself and function correctly. Yet there is a biochemical individuality to us all, so each of us is effected differently by the foods we eat. Poor food choices can produce allergies, lethargy and depression, and increase the chances of developing a chronic illness. The same food that gives Mary a lift may send John spiraling into depression. In the bibliography, you'll find recommended reading on this subject to help you learn more and get more specific about the best food strategies for strengthening your system.

People who eat unwisely tend to make their food choices exclusively in the here and now. People who make wise choices about the food they eat include the big picture consequences of what they're eating in the here and now.

If you break the process of eating down into three simple stages, you can learn alot about what motivates your food choices. Stage one: When to eat. Stage two: What to eat. Stage Three: When to stop. Go through these one at a time, so that you can become conscious of how you're making your choices around food.

Stage One: When to eat

How do you know when to eat? Common reasons include

- time of day

- hunger

- boredom

- to fill an emotional void

- to avoid something else

- attached to another activity (popcorn at the movies, snacking while watching television)

- when others are doing it

- as a reward for doing something else

Stage Two: What to eat?

How do you know what to eat? Common reasons include

- It's healthy

- It's low calorie

- It's low fat

- It tastes good

- It's easy to make

- It's easy to get

- It's a response to stress

- It's the people you are with are eating it

- It evokes a pleasant memory

Stage Three: When to stop

How do you know when to stop eating? Common reasons include

- When the food on the plate is gone

- When one more bite and you will explode

- When your parent have finally stopped saying "eat, eat"

- When you are satisfied

- When it's not as good as you hoped

- When you know if you eat more you will feel uncomfortable

- When you know you don't need anymore food

Some of these reasons to start, choose and stop will be more effective than others in guiding your dietary behavior. If you eat because you're bored, or as a response to stress, and you don't stop until you're about to explode, your experience will be different than if you eat because you're hungry and choose food for its health value, and stop eating before you're full.

The pleasure you get from food is important though, and contributes to your health and well-being. If your short term pleasure causes you long term pain, then at some point your short term pleasure will be eaten by the pain, and then it will be gone. The good news is that it's possible to have your cake, and your health too. We recommend you follow the 80/20 rule. Make 80% of your food choices based on your health and energy, and 20% based on "other criteria". Sally wants to eat a lower fat diet, but she has a desire for a gourmet treat. She realizes that she's going to Las Vegas tomorrow, and Wolfgang Puck has a restaurant there. Instead of having the gourmet treat today, she chooses a simple salad, because tomorrow she will dine.

If you eat to fill an emptiness in your heart, you'll never be able to eat enough. Trying to fill the void with mass quantities of edible substances just doesn't work, unless your goal is weight gain and heartbreak. If your emotional needs are significantly linked to eating, we recommend that you go back to the chapters on Changing your Habits and Learning your Lessons, and find other ways to fulfill your emotional needs that don't require food. Then your fuel stops can support your life by design.

If you want to, you can see how food in general, and what food specifically, effects your energy. Simply chart the trends. In the Inventory' activity of this chapter , we will give you a way to do just that.

COMPELLING FUTURES

*Civilization is a race between education
and catastrophe.
-H.G. Wells*

When a person finds their motivation to change the habitual way they take care of themselves, chances are good that they find it inside of two views of the future, one irresistible, the other repulsive. A future that beckons is like a tractor beam that pulls you forward, while a future that frightens you serves as a repulser ray that pushes you away. Over the course of a lifetime, your hopes and fears will naturally and eventually become clear to you. If the process takes too long, you may find the repulsive future looming on your horizon, and the irresistible one fading from the realm of possibility.

But you don't have to wait for clarity. You can use your imagination to speed up the process now! Compelling futures can be intentionally designed, and the more three dimensional, vivid and intense you make these competing ideas, the more potent they are as internal agents of change.

Some people find it easier to create these compelling futures by writing them down, letting one step lead to the next until the inevitable outcomes of present behavioral choices become apparent. Others are able to bring these futures into focus through a relaxed flight of fancy into their imagination. Still others do best by finding living examples of possible positive and negative futures by looking for others who already made their choices and are living with the consequences. Experiment with this and you will find what works best for you.

For example, if you want to lose weight and gain self esteem, imagine getting older and fatter, see yourself doing nothing more to change and notice how that adds up in the months and years ahead. To enhance the experience, see your future body nude in a mirror, or feel the effort and exertion it takes to move and function. You could even add a sound track of self talk, where your future self says "If only I'd done something back in the past, I wouldn't be in this situation now!" Or, you could spend several weeks closely observing the difficulties that larger people have in moving and getting comfortable in different kinds of chairs, and the way that the people around them look at them, talk to them and treat them. Then observe the energy, ease and grace with which healthy people in your desired weight range move about in society.

Or, you could write a story about your future self, the difficulties you encounter as a result of bad health and bad feelings from being overweight and allowing laziness or stupidity to be the source of your decisions. Write about the choices you made that lead to this awful outcome. Then turn it around. Imagine a positive compelling future, and write a story about that, and include the steps taken, the choices made, the dates and times of turning points that produced the happy ending.

If you want to quit smoking and start breathing deeply, you could imagine yourself in a hospital some years in the future. See the pain in the faces of your loved ones, and consider all that is stolen from their lives and yours because of your habit of breathing smoke instead of air. Feel what it's like to lose your voice and have to talk through a piece of equipment. Contemplate the loss of being able to take a special trip to celebrate a marriage or birth, and your family's loss that results from something you didn't do when there was still time to do something. Add in the pain, sadness, regret and disappointment to make this future extremely unpleasant, and well worth avoiding. A visit to emphysema and lung cancer patients in a hospital near you will make this more vivid for you.

Once the awful future has been seen, look at the steps that led you there, and connect it back to the here and now. Then, immediately take the time to create an alternative future, the one that will happen if the habit is broken, or the behavior changed. Again, the more specific you are about choices and actions, the more depth, color, animation and vibrancy you add, the more compelling these futures will be and the better they will serve you as motivating agents of change.

INVENTORY YOUR EXPERIENCE: LAB STUDIES PART 2

1. Make A Diet Diary

There are plenty of studies to convince even the most cynical member of CPA (Couch Potatoes Anonymous) that a high fiber diet will bring out the best in you. Yet many people tend to make choices about food either in the moment ("hmm, let's see what's on the menu!") or for the near future. To see the big picture of your dietary habits, we recommend a diet diary for tracking the trends.

For several days, write down everything that you eat and drink. Every half hour, give yourself an energy rating. Measure your energy on a scale of 1-10, with 10 as the highest energy rating, 8 for good energy, 6 for just enough energy, 4 meaning that you're kind of tired, 2 representing that you're sleepy, and 0 meaning that you've crashed. This will help you to recognize which food items contribute to high energy and which food items deplete your system. A side effect is that you may discover that you are sensitive to certain foods, that you would be better off to avoid entirely.

2. Make An Exercise Calendar

In the case of exercise, there are certainly enough studies to demonstrate beyond a shadow of a doubt that if you don't use it, you lose it. Clearly, people who exercise regularly live longer, on average, than people who move at the speed of diseased livestock. A wall calendar divided into weeks and days will be revealing. Use either colored pens or colored sticky stars to mark off your progress. Each time that you engage in aerobic exercise, give yourself a gold star or mark, and each time you engage in anaerobic exercise (weight training, for example), give yourself a silver star or mark. Mild exercise (a brief walk around the block) earns you a blue star or mark. And each day in which you do not exercise, color it black.

After you have the overview on your eating and exercise habits, create a project sheet for each health goal. Get a sense of what you want to change and why, name your health project something that interests you, and set a target date for completion.

3. Make A Life List

Make a poster, and create some categories related to changing your energy destroying habits. Every time that you make a wise choice in one of these categories, put a mark on the list. This allows you to have an overview of your overall success, rather than being limited to a particular day's success or failure. If your plan is to exercise frequently, and you didn't do it yesterday or today, you might feel hopeless about changing this behavior. But when you look at the life list and see 5 marks in a row before yesterday, you can realize "Hey, that's 5 out of 7 days!" You can actually gain momentum from keeping track of your successes, as a trickle of change becomes a dynamic stream of events.

Once you've started your diet diary, exercise calendar and life list, join us in the next chapter to learn how to shatter the chains of complacency for a life by design.

Part 3

CHOICES ABOUT ATTITUDES

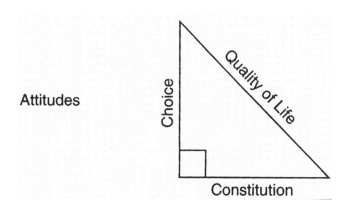

Life is what happens to you while you're busy
making other plans.
-John Lenno

12. MAKING UP YOUR MIND

THE PRINCIPLE OF UNCERTAINTY

The illiterate of the future are not those who cannot read or write. They are those who cannot learn, unlearn, and relearn.
-Alvin Toffler

Contrary to popular concept, uncertainty is not inherently a bad thing. In fact, it is often a doorway to new insights and understanding, and it gives us the opportunity to change things. There is a principle of uncertainty, first articulated by the physicist Werner Heisenberg, who observed experimentally that if a scientist structures experiments to study wave properties of matter at a subatomic level, matter behaves like a wave. If the experiment is designed to examine subatomic particles, matter appears to be present in particle form. So when you look for a particle you find a particle, and when you look for a wave you find a wave, but you never find a particle when looking for a wave. The Uncertainty Principle says that what you look for determines what you find, and that until you look, matter exists as neither particle nor wave, but rather as potential. The experimenter cannot help but influence the results of the experiment.

Translated into human terms, this would seem to imply that your life isn't happening to you, it's happening through you! If you look back over the course of your entire life, you will find that all your experiences have one thing in common: You were there, making decisions, forming opinions, acting as if they were true, and looking for proof. And until you look back, all that is there are sets of potentialities and possibilities.

This is the mind-body connection, the relationship between what you think, what you do, and what you get out of life. In effect, this means that if you believe you are powerless, you will prove it to yourself. And if you believe you can live a life by design, then you will! The principle of uncertainty points to the self fulfilling nature of our lives, for as you believe, so shall it be.

TRYING TO MAKE SENSE

What a distressing contrast there is between the radiant intelligence of the child and the feeble mentality of the average adult.
- Sigmund Freud

If your life is a reflection of your thoughts and attitudes, then it becomes apparent why the mind is a terrible thing to waste! We want to tell you a story about you. Not who you think you are, but the you that was you before you decided who you are, and that will still be you long after you have changed your mind another dozen times. It's the story of the birth of the generalization known as your personality.

Birth: The First Frontier. Your mind may not recall the details, but your nervous system certainly does. You were living in a perfect world. Robin Williams, gifted actor and comedian, once pointed out that a growing fetus has it made, resting in an indoor heated pool and having every need met by womb service. Nothing was required of you except to be and to grow. And you did grow. So much in fact, that this comfortable chamber became too small for you, and you began to stretch against the confines of the ever-more crowding walls. And at some point, you pushed hard enough to trigger a cascade of reactions that led to your birth.

Suddenly, you were in a new place. Big, bright and busy, a new world of raw experience, filling your senses to overflowing, then overwhelming them. Every sight, sound, every everything, was exquisitely new. Try to remember what that's like for a moment. According to modern science, there are at least 7 billion bits of sensory data bombarding your nervous system in every moment of your existence. You tried to pay attention to this sensory bombardment of input and information, and when you could take in no more, you napped. Blobs of experience appeared and disappeared, and after a while, they became familiar to you, as your own feet and toes, and other people! They'd lean in close to you, their faces looming large, as they said "What a cute baby!" Which might as well have been "Boogyboogyboogy...." for all the language you understood.

TUNNELED VISION

There's no idea more dangerous
than the only one you have.
- Anonymous

In a 1956 article, George Miller of the American Psychological Association suggested that the limit of conscious awareness is about seven, plus or minus two, bits of sensory data, our of a field of seven billion possible bits. To navigate your way in this new world, you had to filter and reduce seven billion bits of data down to a digestible seven bits! While anything is psychological if you think about it, here is a profound thought. Whatever you pay attention to with the little spotlight of your conscious awareness keeps you from paying attention to everything else!

Out of an indescribable sea of sensory experiences, you organized your perceptions to recognize and respond to the familiar. With the awakening of your conscious mind, you compared yourself to everything you could identify, and triggered your first identity crisis. Who were you, you wondered, relative to your parents, siblings and peers? Perhaps you decided you were cute, or funny, or unloved, or unimportant. The people around you helped you. They explained things to you, and you to others. Whatever they believed about you, they told you to believe the same. And you did, in your own unique way. This was no easy task, because much of what you were told made very little sense. They told you to 'act your age,' 'mind your manners,' 'watch your mouth,' and 'be on your best behavior.' You did your best to comprehend and respond.

All the while, you were figuring out who you were, and who you were supposed to be. In the creative construction project that became the generalization you call your 'personality,' you made decisions about yourself relative to all sorts of things, like learning, work, love and life itself! Maybe you decided that you were lovable or unlovable, cute or ugly, that babbling was fun , or caused people to yell at you. Maybe you decided that life is a scary place and you'd better feel sorry for yourself, or that you weren't good at certain things, or just weren't good at all. But when you were done, you looked upon your creative construction project, and saw that it was good. Or bad. Or just so-so. But it was yours: A unique set of assumptions about yourself in relationship to everything else.

YOU ARE MORE THAN YOU THINK

*Don't let your education
get in the way of your learning.*
- Mark Twain

The impact of the decisions you've made and assumptions you've formed since your birth have influenced your behavior ever since. To this day, your opinions and beliefs have far more influence over how you deal with change and challenge than the changes and challenges themselves.

The point of all this? While you live in a real world, you do not deal directly or immediately with reality. Instead, you perceive a world of your own making, and act accordingly. While your actions and choices have a real influence on the real world, you are compelled by your nature to observe the consequences of your actions with the primary goal of proving yourself right! This is the uncertainty principle at work. Whatever you assume to be true, you'll act as if it is true, and then look for proof that you're right! There's a huge upside to the self-fulfilling nature of your thoughts and ideas: It offers you a point of leverage through which you can deal with change, meet your challenges, make wise choices and live your life by design.

This leverage becomes available when you recognize that there are two kinds of assumptions by which you can guide your behavior, limiting and useful ones. Limiting assumptions, like 'I'm bad with money' and 'people can't be trusted,' and 'nobody cares,' tie you up, hold you back and trap you into self-defeating and counter-productive behavior. When you experience emotional pain or mental dissatisfaction, quite often it is a limitation in your representation of the world, rather than in the world itself. The 'proof' is in the pudding! Listen sometime to people arguing and you may hear the determination of each party to hold on to their piece of 'truth', to defend it as if their life depends on it. Limiting assumptions tend to carry a heavy price of pain, conflict and suffering.

Then there are useful assumptions, like "I can do whatever I set my mind to" and "Things have a way of working out for the better." These assumptions inform and empower your choices , and then expand the way you pay attention to the effects of those choices. Useful assumptions help us by transforming manure into fertilizer and lemons into lemonade.

GET SERIOUS?

No matter how cynical you get, it's hard to keep up.
- Lily Tomlin

So proving to yourself that you are right is the booby prize in life, and all too often it is the prize that people settle for. Being right requires no wisdom, no commitment, no intelligence. When your life gets bogged down in a field of inertia and lethargy, or your emotions threaten to overwhelm you with anger and unhappiness , a part of you has decided that it needs to be right, in order to have some certainty about what's important enough to take so seriously.

For example: If all you pay attention to is the negativity in the world, that's all you'll see. When you look at the weather, you see it's partly cloudy. When you look at your gas tank, it's half empty. Joe is just such a person. He's a nice guy, but he consistently looks for the dark cloud in every silver lining. One day, Tim takes him out to lunch, to show his appreciation for a referral. He raises his glass and offers a toast: "Hey Joe, here's to you. I appreciate your support for my business." And Joe replies "That's the problem. I never get any appreciation." Tim clears his throat and tries again. "Um...you're getting some now! I appreciate you." And Joe replies "Yeah, I never get that." And he never did.

For some people, the need to be right is so important and so serious that it produces an unhealthy condition of terminal rightness called 'dead serious!' As silly as this may sound, some people would rather be right even if it kills them. Maybe this partly explains the escape clause written into the marriage ceremony: "Til' death do we part.' Rather than changing their mind, making wise choices and meeting the challenges of living their lives by design, some people would rather just die, all at once or a little bit at a time. You can hear it in the language they use to describe their experience of being right, when they say "This is killing me!" or "This job is murder!" or "You stabbed me in the back!" or "You're breaking my heart!"

The pay off for all your assumptions is that you get to prove to yourself how right you are about the people you love, the work that you do, and the way that you live your life. Now if you get to be right about whatever you decide, then what do you want to be right about? If life is self-fulfilling by nature, then into what ideas and assumptions do you want to invest your life's energy? It is in the an-

swer to these simple questions that you are blessed or burdened with the creative opportunity of living your life by design.

INVENTORY YOUR EXPERIENCE: SEEING WHAT YOU THINK

Here is your opportunity to finish some of the chapters in the unfinished story of your life. Take some time to examine your assumptions and opinions about the following questions, and see whether they have limited you and/or empowered you in the way your life is turning out. In other words, in the experiment that is your life, what did you look for and what did you find? What are the decisions you made back then that you've been proving yourself right about ever since?

Review Past Decisions

What did you decide about yourself in relation to your parents?

What did you decide about yourself in relation to your siblings?

What did you decide about yourself in relation to your peers?

What did you decide about them (parents, siblings, peers)?

What did you decide about your ability to learn something new?

What did you decide about the meaning and nature of work?

What did you decide about how lovable you are?

What did you decide about life itself, its meaning and purpose?

Answer these questions in detail, to the best of your ability, and then join us in the next chapter, where we'll explore how to use your mind on purpose to shatter the chains of complacency.

13. SHATTERING YOUR CHAINS

NUMB AND NUMBER

Restlessness and discontent
are the necessities of progress.
- Thomas A. Edison

Perhaps you are feeling a little overwhelmed by all this information, by all these calls to 'inventory your experience', with the whole concept of a life by design.   After all, if you just let things slide, don't they always have a way of working themselves out anyway?   Isn't it really enough to just get by from day to day?   Perhaps you've started to wonder why you should care enough to give your very best to the way your life turns out?

Statesman Patrick Henry had an answer to that question.   In his famous speech he spoke out against the complacent do-nothings of his time, when he said " Why stand we here idle?   What is it the gentlemen want?   What would they have?   Is life so dear, is peace so sweet, as to be purchased at the price of chains and slavery? Forbid it, almighty God. I know not what course others may take, but as for me, give me liberty or give me death!" His meaning was clear: Complacency is a form of slavery, binding one to a living death of inaction, non participation and default. The shackles are easy to slip into. They're comfortable chains at first, because they require nothing but your disinterest and indifference.

FIXING TO DIE

It's not that I am afraid of death,
I just don't want to be there when it happens..
- Woody Allen

The idea that death is better than life has proliferated on earth since the beginning of time, perpetuated and promoted by those who gain most from the complacency of others. This idea is rooted in often unexamined assumptions about what happens when someone dies. So people who are more afraid to live than they are to die, and who assume that death is the certain end of everything, can look forward to death as a way out of the uncertainty and difficulty of life. For others, death is the promise of a second chance to be with loved ones, or a promise that they go to live with God. Of course this assumes that there is a heaven into which they will gain admittance, because they've said the magic words or done the works as directed by their religious leaders. And then there are those who see death as the opportunity to get a fresh start, based on the assumption that reincarnation is a guarantee. We make no claim of special knowledge about what awaits on the other side of life. But we have seen these comfortable or comforting assumptions become traps, and lives become cages in which people die, never having truly lived.

Speaking of croaking, perhaps you recall the Bateson frog experiment? Here's how it was explained to us. Scientists, under the direction of famed psychologist Gregory Bateson, created an artificial frog

143

pond with a heating element beneath it. Then they raised tadpoles in this controlled environment. When the tadpoles had become frogs, the scientists began to turn up the heat, one degree at a time. They were curious to know at what temperature the frogs would perceive the danger and leap to safety. This is what they found: At no point did the frogs perceive the danger. They simply continued to adapt to the increasing temperature until the heat had slowed them down and made it impossible for them to move. How similar that is to the complacent people who make their little adaptations in order to stay put and avoid change. Like the unfortunate frogs, they kill themselves by kidding themselves!

The frogs apparently failed to notice the temperature change. But what if some frog-loving scientists had taken paddles and raised an alarm by whacking the surface of the pond, or turned the temperature up really fast so the change would be more noticeable? Perhaps they could have frightened the frogs into leaping to safety before they were completely cooked.

Complacent people ignore the warning signs, until life itself whacks the pond and forces them to change, because earthquakes, war, fires and floods are insistent reminders about the precious nature of life. But why wait for disaster to whack your pond, when you can wake yourself and keep yourself awake? Isn't that better than a rude awakening from the slumber of your contented discontent?

USE IT OR LOSE IT

Don't it always seem to go, that you
don't know what you've got til' it's gone.
- Joni Mitchell

Our inactions have consequences. Making the easy choice in the moment and doing what's most convenient at the time almost always leads to complications and trouble, a soap opera whose happy endings are fleeting setups for more difficulty and travail. When creative energy is inhibited and suppressed by avoidance and denial, the result is unconscious and self-defeating behavior that guarantees a future shock.

Whenever your life force is at a low ebb, the lack of energy and motion is a sign that your innate creativity is atrophying along with the rest of you. Like food left in the freezer too long , or a vintage wine turned to vinegar, everything on earth eventually goes into decay. To keep life fresh, you've got to make a little positive trouble now and then, stir the pot, thaw the food, pop the cork, rattle the cage, move it intentionally or lose it! Creative living stands out against the darkness of time, surrounded by the light of progress. As individuals, family members, and shareholders in communities, the use of our creative energy aimed at better tomorrows is self renewing, in that it allows us to slip the bonds of earth and soar to the heights of our hopes and dreams.

What can be done? Some people spend their whole lives waiting for something to come along, some project or vision or relationship to ignite their passion and move them to action. While their lives are on hold, they make unwise choices that interfere with happiness and fulfillment. The simple truth is that you are more likely to find the something that you're waiting for while you are doing something productive. To keep good things from going bad, you've got to go against the grain of your complacency sometimes, and intentionally make a little trouble for yourself, go out of your way, push the envelope, make the harder choice and do what needs to be done!

At the very foundation of your life, there is a basic desire waiting to ignite into action. That is the desire to make a meaningful difference with your life, to have your life count for something worthwhile. A life lived in creative freedom is filled with courageous action. The world has many needs, including a need for you to get involved. Whether you join a movement to change the world, or start one yourself, from recycling, to housing the homeless, to building habitats for humanity, the opportunities are vast to slip the bonds of lethargy that make you part of the problem and add your creative energy to creating the solution.

INVENTORY YOUR EXPERIENCE: RIPPLE EFFECT

Now, it's time to take this personally! What follows are several suggestions for rousing yourself from the boredom and illusion of security, and shattering the chains of complacency.

Go Your Own Way

The Ashland Bakery and Cafe in southern Oregon uses the slogan ' Life is short. Eat dessert first!' It is a potent message to stop waiting and get on with the good stuff in life! You can break the 'always the same way' habit, and go a different way, even if it is the longer way, just for the sake of curiosity! Take a road less traveled, one that has the same general direction as the direction you're going, only you have no idea where it goes. Because there's no telling what you'll find until you've found it. (Warning: Do this on a full tank of gas!)

Observe yourself for the next 24 hours, and identify those areas of your life where you have been asleep at the wheel. Identify those grooves in your life that have become ruts. Where do you automate your behavior? Which section of the bookstore, library or magazine shop do you habitually visit first? Which television shows do you watch that are most conducive to your being a couch potato? Where have you stopped paying attention?

You can take any habitual behavior and break up the routine, just to see what happens. You can clear your desk each day into an empty drawer, and then start over. You can rearrange the items on the wall of your house, move kitchen items into a different cabinet arrangement, you can even get dressed in the opposite order! Of course, that will require you to first determine the order in which you dress yourself. Make a list, then rework the list and see if you can get dressed in the new order without backsliding to the tried and true!

Ready Fire Aim

Too much planning destroys spontaneity and interferes with creative thinking. There is much to be said for taking action, and taking it NOW instead of later. Any thing that you have to sit around thinking about, planning, budgeting for, organizing to create, chances are that it will lack the thrust needed to overcome the inertia built into your system. The fact is that it takes more power and energy for lift off and clearing the earth's gravitational pull than it does to navigate around the planet for a million miles and return safely to earth. Lacking an inviting target, sometimes pushing yourself forward anyway is enough to get events moving and increase the range of objects in your radar! There is a kind of momentum that accrues when one suddenly changes careers, moves to a new town, adopts a child, or starts a new painting.

Shift Your Gears

Some people are chronically stuck in second gear, others keep the pedal to the metal at all times. Sometimes all that's needed is to shift the gears in order to break free of the traction of habitual living. Finding opportunities for alternate rhythms is an excellent way to get your life force moving. When you've been rushing all day, a slow walk helps you regain your balance. And when you've been putting one foot methodically in front of another all day long, you can go dancing and delight yourself with your fancy footwork. Been quiet too long? Go to the forest or the beach and let out a few yells! Been yelling to overcome a noisy backdrop? Read quietly to yourself as compensation.

Ask Stupid Questions

Buckminster Fuller once said "Dare to be naive." It is the limitless curiosity of a child that opens doors to new insights, that fuels their vast supply of energy, that makes it possible for them to learn and grow at such a fevered pace. A curious child doesn't hesitate to ask 'Why do you do that?' or 'Why do you do that like that?' You too can become like the children, and keep your energy and enthusiasm alive, awake, and alert. Instead of settling for easy answers, seek to know more. Challenge undeserved authority with your curiosity, challenge arrogance with innocence, and look for ways to make little improvements in all you do by asking yourself frequently, "Why do I do this like this?" And when you've found your answer, ask "Is there another way that might work even better than this?" And if it ain't broke, as the saying goes, break it! You just may find that you're breaking a shell that has enclosed your understanding.

Odd, isn't it?

Instead of trodding the familiar paths, or watching to see which way the wind will blow, you can cultivate odd hobbies, read odd stuff, engage in activities that give you new perspective. Purposefully step outside the boundaries of your former existence, become fascinated with and examine more closely those people, places and things at variance your idea of normal. Ever notice how you gravitate towards the same part of the bookstore? Go to the opposite side and read something you never would have thought of reading before! Always dial in the same radio station? Go to the opposite end of the spectrum! Do you read a newspaper daily? Try going a week without, and find other ways to find out what's going on. That person that seems so peculiar to you? Take them to lunch, and find out how they work!

Reading these suggestions makes little difference. To truly invigorate yourself for a life by design, you must take action. Life is not a spectator sport, which means that you've got to get involved if you want to play. Whatever method you choose to shake yourself free of the numbness of complacency, do it now. because tomorrow never comes for those who wait until tomorrow for what is best done today!

14. NEUTRALIZING NEGATIVITY

IT'S A STUPID STUPID WORLD

Garbage in. Garbage out.
- Computer programming principle

Every moment of every day, you're subjected to a continuous bombardment of global stupidity. It comes at you through the many communication channels that connect our modern world. Psychic garbage for mass consumption, the nightly broadcast of murder and mayhem is enough to terrify the soul, and make the human mind run wild with fear based fantasies. The sirens that blare, the rocket's red glare in wars and rumors of wars, famine and earthquake in diverse places. And wherever you look, whenever you listen, whatever you do, the world around you is often noisy, dirty, filled with wretchedness and heartache.

The computer principle now applies to people, because it is now perfectly clear: Garbage in, garbage out. How does our society cope with all the negativity? Whenever the feelings of anger or sadness come up, you can stuff them with food, or drink, or drugs, or turn on the televisions set to see it again, or find some other diversion from the truth that you know your life and world could be, should be more. People under the influence of negativity make excuses, the most common being "I'm not negative, I'm just realistic."

It doesn't have to be that way. It's really up to you. What do you want to fill your life with? If you put your head into an enclosed space filled with loud music and bad news, eventually your head will ache. If you fill yourself up with sources of positive thought and uplifting ideas, eventually you'll start seeing the world that way. In other words, if you stick your head in a cold mountain stream, sooner or later you will wake up!

Victor Frankel, who wrote about Holocaust survivors in his book 'Man's Search For Meaning,' said this: "...everything can be taken from a man but one thing: the last of human freedoms - to choose one's attitude in any given set of circumstances - to choose one's own way." In our experience with patients who have turned their lives around after abysmally bad experiences, we've observed some attitudes that seem to reverse the tide of negativity before it washes everything away.

ATTITUDE ADJUSTMENTS

Be happy while you're living,
for you're a long time dead.
- Scottish Proverb
Accept The Unacceptable

One way to collapse into a depressed heap of negativity is to compare what you have to what you don't have. Remember these two simple sayings: You get what you resist. So go for what you want, but want what you get. Acceptance isn't acquiescence, but until you see beyond the 'this is good, this is bad' polarity, you cannot see things for what they are, face them and deal with them effectively. You cannot solve a problem, until you stop fighting it or withdrawing from it, and face it squarely. Instead of hating the bad and fixating on it, open your mind and heart to the possibility that the problems of the world are vehicles for change and contribution.

Forgiveness

According to Brandon St. John, you live what you can't forgive. We have also found this to be true in our work with people who have recovered from traumatic interpersonal experiences and gone on to fulfilling and meaningful lives. To live in the present, you must relinquish the burdens of the past. Fail to learn the lesson of a difficult experience and it keeps coming back around. The circumstances change, but the lesson repeats. This accounts for the haunted quality you may have observed in people who can't let go of their grievances against themselves and others. When you hold on to past grievances against others, you associate yourself with what is no longer happening, and thus dissociate you from what is real. When the past defines the space, there's no room for a fresh view. It is only human to make a mistake, but to forgive is divinely human.

Consider the nature of blame: In this adversarial approach to life, whenever you point a finger at someone or something outside yourself, you have a few fingers pointing back at you. That means that in the act of blaming, you make an effect out of yourself, instead of being the cause of an effect. And it isn't possible to be the cause of an effect when you are the effect of what is changing. Some people have told us that blame actually feels good, if they say it loud and back it with emotional force. These are generally the nice people, the calm people, the quiet and amiable people, people who keep their feelings under wraps while doing a slow burn. They can get a brief improvement in how they feel by releasing all their anger, and telling the truth about where they place the blame for what isn't working in their lives. But the benefit is short lived, because shortly after losing it, these same people will be filled with self-loathing and embarrassment, hating themselves for having told the truth. Blaming is a short term solution that offers no meaningful long-term result.

Forgiveness is based, at least in part, on the recognition that everyone in life is using trial and error to learn just like you, their role models may not have been up to the task, and they're doing the best they can with the limited resources they have on board. The abused becomes the abuser, and the accused becomes the accuser, so when you can't forgive others their trespasses, you may have the same problem with yourself. You can be your own worst critic, but not as long as you're criticizing someone else. Take your judgments off of others and you'll likely find your own shortcomings and self blame staring back at you.

We see this in the behavior of nations towards one another. A cousin, Terry, was serving with the U.N. peacekeeping forces in Bosnia, and in an email he reported a curious fact. He found that, rather than being pleased that the warring had stopped, that their children could walk in safety down a street, the factions in this fractured nation continued to want revenge for injustices done hundreds of years earlier. And the irony was that these people who hated one another dressed alike, looked alike, talked alike, and even hated alike.

Of course this pattern of promoting negativity by clinging to the pain of the past exists in every troubled corner of the globe, from Ireland to India to Israel, from Peru to Pakistan, and in dozens of other hot spots between and within nations around the world. That tells you something about the history of humanity, where the failure to learn the lessons of the past keeps dooming us to repeating them, and where the grave danger grows as the weaponry improves. It also shows that what you can't forgive, you live, because health, education and social needs are neglected in order to pay for the conflict. As Indira Gandhi said, you can't shake hands with a clenched fist. While countries, like individuals, can learn to see their neighbors with greater understanding and tolerance for differences, it doesn't happen on its own. It requires acts of courageous will to let go of the need for

153

revenge.

Every negative experience is an opportunity for you to learn something about yourself, your character and your values. Learn from the experience, make the pain of the past worthwhile, and you will have protected yourself from experiencing it again.

Be Receptive To Good

Giving and receiving are two sides of a single experience. One cannot exist without the other. A transmitter is useless without a receiver. And a gift has little value unless someone opens it. Yet in times of challenge and times of need, tis' easier to give than to receive. Many people who have depended on public assistance to get back on their feet say that it feels degrading to accept the charity of others. Yet their receiving of the gifts of society was in itself a gift to the givers, because it gave them a place to make a difference!

You must be receptive to the good in life, or it can't get in. Do you know someone who is unable to receive a simple compliment? You say "What a lovely outfit!" and they reply, "Oh, it's just some old thing I had in the closet." It is as if they want to kill the gift of good before it affects them!

For the receptive person, fortuitous circumstance is a frequent event. Call these experiences gifts of grace if you like, but there are moments when something wonderful happens that affirms you and helps you along. When such moments present themselves, you've got to be receptive, open to the moment of inspiration out of which the grace can flow.

Out there, somewhere, in the uncharted reaches of interconnections and relationships that you've yet to encounter, there are opportunities undreamed of and positive side effects still unimagined by you. As an antidote for negativity, receptivity is the attitude of being open to a good that is yet to be.

CONTEMPLATE THE POSSIBLE

Some look at things that are not and ask why,
I ask 'Why not?'
- Robert Kennedy

Anything is possible. At every juncture in human history, someone has been there to say that the possible is impossible. Yet every
great breakthrough came in to being because someone believed in
the possible. When you believe that something is so and can be
achieved, you gain the confidence to choose a course of action. When
you believe that it cannot be done, you lose confidence, and whatever
action you happen to take will be undermined by your certainty that
you can define the future by the limitations of the past.

Try this instead: Think and act "as if' a better future is possible.
Allow yourself to consider at every step of the way how you would
proceed if you knew something was not just possible but probable,
then act as if you have already possess this knowledge. You'll find
time and again that acting 'as if' causes the the improbable to become the probable and the impossible to become the possible.

'As if' thinking works great to reverse the negativity caused by
the fear that something will get worse. Move forward 'as if' things
are going to get better, as if your problem will be solved. You will
find that resources and opportunities come quickly into view, when
you pay attention to your circumstance as if the breakthrough is just
around the corner.

Keep It In Perspective

All things must pass. The long view of history shows us this is
true, from prehistoric creatures to the rise and fall of great civiliza-

tions. For each moment you spend bemoaning the past and worrying about lost opportunities, that is one more precious, irreplaceable moment in the present that has been squandered.

When his teenage son called home after totaling his car, Alan Kirschner sighed and said to himself '100 years from now, what difference will it make?' He went an entire century into the future in order to regain his perspective, because he learned that the size of a problem is diminished by time. Simone Brinkman was once a twin at Auschwitz, and just missed meeting the notorious Nazi Dr. Mengele, nicknamed the Angel of Death because of his cruel experiments on twins. Now if she finds herself troubled about something, she finds that reading a page or two in a book about him puts in perspective whatever is going on in her life right now. She knows that you can always compare what is to something worse to diminish the hold of a difficulty. When times are tough, the human mind is uniquely equipped to go to another time or another place in space and time to regain perspective,.

Life is an adventure with lessons all along the way. If everything was all cherries & roses, we wouldn't have the opportunity to deepen our lives and understanding. Some of your greatest breakthroughs in life have come through lessons learned through adversity. Those are the times and places where we see the stuff of which we're made.

A person is not a failure as a result of the ups and downs of life. What a waste to lose perspective and make mountains out of mole-hills , when your life is but a moment in the great eternity of being .

Be Grateful For Everything

Counting blessings is not just a good idea, it's a great one. By doing this on a regular basis, your soul will be nourished in the recognition of all the good that already exists in your life. Rather than taking good for granted, get good with gratitude, because appreciation of the moment's gifts is essential to happiness. Even in awful moments, counting one's blessings makes a difference. In 'Man's Search For

Meaning,' Victor Frankel describes gratitude for something as small as a glimpse of nature amidst the horror of a concentration camp as a survival factor. To assume that you'll always have another moment, a better moment than this one, is just plain foolish. Our lives can be changed completely in the twinkling of an eye by a crashing comet, a runaway vehicle, or a bad turn down a flight of stairs. The lives of the people we hold dearest exist for certain in this moment alone. Gratitude is a heart opening emotion, and as we allow ourselves to filled by its power, we are nourished and renewed. Indeed, the Greek word for nourishment also means 'to cherish.' The attitude of gratitude allows us to wrap ourselves around this moment, to be renewed in our souls and strengthened for the challenges of life that lie ahead.

When our lives seem not to be going so well in some particular regard, we still have much to be grateful for if we stop to count the blessings. Life's moving pretty fast. If you don't stop and look around, you could miss it. Appreciation in each now moment will make you relax, feel good, and have more energy for leading a fulfilling life in an often neurotic world.

INVENTORY YOUR EXPERIENCE: PUT IT IN WRITING

Now it's your turn to neutralize the negativity in your life. While it can be tremendously therapeutic to talk out loud about your emotional wounds to someone capable of listening well, the person who most needs to hear and understand your pain is you. A bit of letter writing can make emotional resolution easier to achieve when a cloud of negativity hovers over you. Allow yourself to think of at least three people with whom you have a negative history and for whom you still harbor some resentment or dislike. You're going to have an opportunity to write a letter to each of these people, and pour out your negative feelings into words on a page, without censoring any of it. WARNING! Never mail these letters. With this in mind, if you've made up your mind to neutralize negative energy from past grievances with others, here are three emotions, guilt, grief and anger, whose negativity can be transformed for your own well being through letter writing.

Turn Guilt Into Acceptance

To let go of a thing, you must first acknowledge it is there. Facing the good, the bad and the ugly of your past is the beginning of wisdom if you are to learn from your mistakes. Write a letter in which you accept your past actions for what they were, seeing that you were doing the best you could with the limited resources you had on board . Write about what you've learned from the experience, and then write about your determination to give yourself another chance.

Turn Grief Into Release

Grief is the holding on to pictures of what was and is no more. Release comes when we see what it was, see that it is no more, and then say good bye to what can not be. Write a letter in which you say goodbye to all that will never be. Again, do not mail this letter.

Turn Anger Into Forgiveness

You live what you cannot forgive. Anger at another often disguises anger at ourselves for a lack of wisdom or resourcefulness. To forgive another, you must see that they, just like you, were doing the best they could with the limited resources they had on board. But that is impossible until you get all that nastiness out of your system. Write a letter in which you say every rotten thing you can think of to hold that person accountable for your unhappiness. Blame, yell, curse, and if necessary, exhaust yourself in holding this person accountable for how your life turned out.

Once you've written these letters, burn them, and begin one more letter in which you acknowledge that, while the relationships was not what you would have preferred, it has given you valuable life lessons for which you are grateful. Describe what those lessons are and how your experiences in those relationships will serve you in the future . Mailing this kind of letter is optional!

Take these actions, then join us in the next chapter, to learn about dealing with the inherent adversity of life using heart, action and humor!

15. DEALNG WITH ADVERSITY

TRIUMPH IN TRAGEDY

Avoiding danger is no safer in the long run than outright exposure. Life is either a daring adventure, or nothing.
To keep our faces toward change and behave like free spirits in the presence of fate is strength undefeatable.
- Helen Keller

We've said it before and we'll say it again. Life is hard on planet earth, and the signs of the difficulty of living are visible as drinking, drugs, divorce, and disease. No matter how well you plan, no matter how deep you love, life is risky business. Sooner or later, every person will have to deal with some circumstance that seems impossible to bear. Indeed, waking up in the morning and carrying on with the day can be a tremendous act of courage when your life seems filled with adversity.

In conversations with patients, in the letters and email we've received from people who read our previous book, or listened to our tapes, or heard us speak about living lives of purpose and meaning, we have heard incredible tales of suffering and pain, and occasionally a desperate cry for magic answers that will set their world right. While we have no magic answers to take away the difficulty of life, we can offer this meaningful pattern for finding triumph in tragedy. People who successfully deal with their difficulties don't let them run their lives. Instead, they make the decision to live the best life they can in spite of the difficulty. They bounce back from the death of a loved one or a crippling disease by finding their faith and courage in their commitment to living a meaningful life. They bounce back from betrayal and divorce by committing themselves to a deeper knowledge of intimacy and love. They bounce back from business reversals by learning all they can from their experience and applying it to their next step.

They do these things without excuses and justifications for staying stuck in reaction to what was. Instead, they integrate the pain and hardship into the fabric of who they are, allowing their past to inform their present and build their character. We know people who survived life in concentration camps by devoting themselves to the idea of that the best revenge is a life well lived! "They sought to destroy me, and instead, they gave me the will to live!" In many ways, it seems, more is required and more is possible from the person to whom much hardship has been given.

When you let go of fighting and withdrawing from adversity, you're left with change and choice. While you may have no say over what happens to you, you do have a say in what you do with it. Starting with what is and then focusing forward, it is possible to invest the least time and energy in suffering, and the most time and energy in living a life by design.

YOU GOTTA HAVE HEART

Aim at heaven and you get earth thrown in. Aim at earth and you get neither. -C. S. Lewis

While you cannot make the difficulty of life go away, we can offer you something to say when faced with adversity. It isn't a magic word, but it is a word of power. Have you ever said 'Someday I'm going to look back and laugh at this'? Well, why wait? Since you have no guarantees of any tomorrow anyway, since this moment may be the only moment you get, there is no better time than right now to proclaim your power in this moment! And the word is HAH! If you say it aloud, several times in a row really fast, you will recognize it as the sound of laughter. HAH! If you're thinking, 'That's too simple!' then allow us to make it a bit more complicated for you. The word of power is actually an acronym made up of the first letter of three words of power, Heart, Action and Humor.

The first letter stands for Heart! According to the dictionary, the heart is a chambered, muscular organ in vertebrates that pumps blood received from the veins into the arteries, thereby maintaining the flow of blood through the entire circulatory system. The dictionary says there is a similarly functioning structure in invertebrates, which means that even the spineless have a heart!

But the qualities of the heart are numerous. We know that if you don't have your heart in the right place, it makes it hard for you to talk straight. If you heart is in your throat it's hard to talk. If you wear your heart on your sleeve, your fashion statement may invite abuse. But if you have your heart in the right place, you'll be able to find it when you need it. A heavy heart can weigh you down and make it hard to get up again. You're either living with all your heart, or you're half hearted and it's hard to get anything started. And when you say someone has a lot of heart, we mean that they demonstrate the capacity for sympathy, generosity, compassion, love, and courage.

To cultivate these qualities of Heart, you must identify with your humanity! Instead of carrying around your judgments about your fellow human beings, see them instead as the courageous and sympathetic characters they are, struggling against the odds, fighting their fears, overcoming their challenges, learning to love. When you can see these things in others, you will find them in yourself.

Commit to Action

"When you were born, you cried and the world rejoiced. Live your life so that when you die, the world cries and you rejoice." -Native American Saying

In this age of information, there are books and tapes and seminars and personal coaches for just about everything. An attendee at a speech on finding and keeping a mate approached the speaker and said "I thought you looked familiar! I bought your tape!" The speaker replied "I'm delighted." "I'm not!" said the attendee. "It didn't work!" The speaker, hoping it was a mechanical problem, said "If it won't go around and around on your tape player, send it back! I'm sure the publisher will send you a replacement." "Oh, it went around and around all right" she said. "Only I still haven't found my mate!" "Well, said the speaker, I have some good news and some bad news for you. The good news is that that tape program has a one year guarantee!" "What's the bad news?" the attendee replied. "The bad news is that watching that tape will change nothing for you. The only thing that changes anything is your commitment to action, your willingness to do something with what you know, and to do it now!"

When it comes to knowledge, you could say in all honesty that people are full of it, because they take in information but do nothing to put it to use! Can you think of one thing that you know for certain would make your life better in a significant way, yet you still haven't gotten around to actually doing it? Can you think of one thing that you know of a certainty would make your life significantly better if you stopped doing it, yet you continue to do it? Of course you can. Clearly, it isn't what you know, it's also what you do with what you know that counts.

When your life becomes stagnated, sitting around and dwelling on it does little to get things moving again. Instead, you need less time thinking about life, and more time actually living it! There is a tendency that some people have to first think something through, then deliberate on their deliberations, then concern themselves with the problems their deliberations have revealed, until the only thing they can expect of themselves is to do NO thing. The inertia that results from this kind of analysis paralysis can often be prevented and cured by taking one step forward instead of thinking about it one more time.

Tom Peters, in his book 'In Search Of Excellence, ' found that organizations that pursued and achieved excellence had 'a bias for action.' We find that the same holds true for individuals. When faced with resistance, a quick start mentality can dispel the inertia and lead to bold results. As an alternative to being stopped by the enormity of a challenge or the difficulty of a decision, the effective person looks for that one step that can be taken immediately to move through the resistance and overcome the obstacle. The ineffective person sees a problem as a wall and contemplates why nothing can be done, whining and making excuses until the moment of action passes. When faced with the challenges of life, look for that one step forward, that one thing you CAN do, right now, to change the tide of events, at least a little bit. Remember that the side effects of committed action produce new waves of change, and do something now!

Humor is Healthy

Never give up. And never, under any circumstances,
face the facts.
-Ruth Gordon

In the book of proverbs, we read "A joyful heart is good medicine, but a broken spirit dries up the bones" What this means is that if you can't take a joke, you'll wind up on medication. Funny, isn't it? To laugh in the face of despair, you've got to lighten up. The opposite of light is darkness, and the opposite of lightness is gravity. So it figures that the opposite of gloom and heaviness is the lightness of being produced by laughter! That's why laughter is good medicine.

Whenever you have a good laugh, your body secretes natural pain killers called endorphins, known in scientific terms as 'Joy Juice.' Similar to morphine, endorphins are hundreds of times more powerful. In the growing field of psychoneuroimmunology (psycho=the mind, neuro=the nervous system, immuno=the immune system), studies show that while depression weakens the immune system and thus makes people more susceptible to illness, laughter strengthens the immune system to ward off illness, and to defend you whenever you're ill.

Workplace studies show that meetings which begin with healthy laughter are more creative and productive than those which are stiflingly serious. The mere sound of laughter can be nourishing to the soul. Listen to the laughter of children and you may hear the sound of heaven. And watch their delight when they make the grownups laugh! "How do you catch a rabbit? Simple! Hide behind a tree and make sounds like a carrot!" The positive emotions of good humor give you the resilience to bounce back from difficulty, to overcome the gravity of a difficult situation, and to carry you over seemingly insurmountable obstacles.

That's the power of laughter. Watch an audience leaving a comedy club, and if the comedy is good, the people truly leave feeling better! Comedy takes those things which we find perplexing, frustrating and hard to deal with, and finds the humor in them. You are blessed to be living in a time of abundant comedy, with internet sites, radio stations, television shows, magazines, newspapers and clubs devoted to it! Comedians seem determined to expand the envelope of acceptable topics and language as far as possible, making the funny stuff uncomfortable stuff for the stuffy and self righteous . No subject is off limits, and much of it is rude and crude, as comedians take on the full range of human foolishness, arrogance and hypocrisy, from racism to sexism, and every other 'ism' in between. In so doing, comedians are providing a tremendous service to humanity (or at least for those who watch and listen). By helping us to associate good feelings to awful difficulties, to laugh at our ignorance, superstition and fears,they make it easier to think creatively and proactively about changing our condition.

To put all this in perspective, consider that being born is like jumping off a 50 story building. You can either watch the ground rapidly approaching and drop dead of a heart attack halfway down, or you can look around, enjoy the view and say 'So far, so good!' While the end is near in any moment, how you take the ride of life is really

up to you. Adversity builds character, and it does so faster if you remember the word of power! HAH!

INVENTORY YOUR EXPERIENCE: REMIX THE TRACK

1. You Know Who They Are. Make a list of the worst people you've ever known personally. What don't you know about them that might explain their behavior to you in a new way? What would you need to know about each of these people in order to feel compas-

sion for them, or see them as courageous, in spite of their bad behavior?

2. Take Aim For Change. Make a goal and plan for any behavior change that you've known about for more than a year, and yet have not followed through to make it happen.

3. Lighten Up. Make a laughter resource list. Write down the names of everyone you can think of who makes you laugh, or knows how to bring a smile to your face. Keep this list handy for the next time when gravity of a situation starts getting you down, and you need a little lift.

Take these actions, and then join us in the next chapter , where you can turn your mistakes into opportunities for learning.

16. MAKING SOME PROGRESS

MISTAKE MYSTIQUE

Nowadays, most people die of a sort of
creeping common sense,
and discover when it is all too late, that the only
thing one never regrets are one's mistakes.
- Oscar Wilde

Did you get to where you are by doing everything right the first time? A principle of creativity is what Bucky Fuller called the 'Mistake Mystique.' He described this principle by saying that people have "a left foot and a right foot, to make a mistake first to the left, then to the right, left again and repeat." Throughout human history, the pattern holds true. We go too far to the left, then too far to the right, and eventually we make progress. It isn't just people that work this way. Physics has found that the whole universe contains no straight lines, and waves everywhere.

Some days, when you put on your 'I know what I'm doing' outfit, you hope nobody calls you on it because you know that you don't know what you're doing. You're guessing, and a lot of the time you guess wrong. But if you don't take your best shot and see what happens, nothing ever changes. To live creatively, you've got to risk being wrong, risk making mistakes, or nothing interesting and worthwhile can happen.

Playing it safe is probably the single biggest barrier to creative living, and it does seem reasonable at first glance. Taking charge over your life, thinking creatively and acting on the courage of your convictions has proven to be a road less traveled for good reasons, the least of which is the narrow-minded and sometimes hostile reception awaiting you from those who are invested in maintaining the status quo!

Darwin must have known this, when he held back his theory of natural selection for twenty years. He wrote to a friend that "It is like confessing to a murder" because of the certain fear that he would be attacked for his discoveries.

It was with smug certainty that in 1898, the head of the US Patent Office tried to have the patent office closed down, because, as he testified before Congress, 'Everything that can be invented, has been invented.'

Executives at Decca Recording Company rejected the Beatles in 1962, because, as they said, "We don't like their sound, and guitar music is on it's way out.

Steve Jobs and Steve Wozniak didn't know exactly how it would turn out. They just wanted to develop their ideas about a personal computer. They would have given it away in exchange for the chance to work on the project. But the two Steves were turned away by both Atari and Hewlett Packard, because they seemed too young to know what they were talking about, and hadn't finished college! So the personal computer was born in a garage, and launched the revolution that gave computing power to 'the rest of us.'

History is rife with examples of free thinking and courageous people with good ideas and bold goals who initially got nothing but the cold shoulder and chilly looks. Movies that talked, the telephone, the television, the automobile, and the airplane were all met with disbelief and irritation .

Tolstoy wrote: "I know that most men, including those at ease with problems of the greatest complexity, can seldom accept even the simplest and most obvious truth if it be such as would oblige them to admit the falsity of conclusions which they have delighted in explaining to colleagues, which they have proudly taught to others, and which they have woven, thread by thread, into the fabric of their lives."

CHARTING A CREATIVE COURSE

I used to think the people who were weird were weird. I suddenly realized that the people who were weird weren't weird at all. It was the people who were saying they were weird that were weird.
- Sir Paul McCartney

We are all unique. You cannot be duplicated. You must find your own way, define your best effort and act on it with the conviction that your life can and will be fulfilling.   You learn, then you refine those learnings. You balance your short term happiness with your long term health and well being. Though help is available, ultimately change is a pathway that must be followed with courage.

In ancient days, livestock trails became well worn paths. In time, these paths were paved over and turned into roads. Now, with everything in flux, it often makes sense to stop paving the cow paths. Sometimes, as Michael Hammer advised, we should obliterate the cow paths and start over! Instead of blindly following trails that lead to nowhere in particular, you can see uncertainty as a doorway to new opportunities. To live creatively is to take risks in pursuit of bold goals. The people who change things tend to be the discontented ones who have grand ideas about what is possible and no concept of

170

the difficulties they may face in bringing their dreams to life. To be an agent of change, you've got to think different.

INVENTORY YOUR EXPERIENCE: WAVY LINES

1. Learn From Your Mistakes. Take the time to describe the biggest mistakes you've made in your life to date, what you've learned from those mistakes, and how this learning has given you the informed perspective to get to where you are in your life right now.

2. Recall Your Bright Ideas. Remember some of your own bright ideas that have been dismissed by others, and areas of life you were curious about that later became of interest to others.

Once you've completed listing and evaluating the learning moments of your past, you will have completed this section on the changing world you live in, and you can consider yourself to be a current event! Then join us in the next chapter of the book where we will look at the positive assumptions of people who are successful at living their life by design.

17. CULTIVATING HEALTHY ATTITUDES

Useful Assumptions

The real voyage of discovery consists not in seeking new lands, but in seeing with new eyes.
- Marcel Proust

Since a life of personal renaissance is based on useful assumptions, we've collected a list of simple assumptions that have proven themselves to be useful in helping people increase the quality of their lives. They are each a part of a general attitude of approach to life rather than avoidance of it. Try them on for size. Imagine the kind of choices you can make based on assumptions such as these:

1. No matter the situation, there is more to life than you perceive.

Because of the limitations on your conscious ability to pay attention, there will always be more going on than the little bit you notice. When you feel stuck and can't see your way out of a situation, question your assumptions, challenge your generalizations, then look around. Then find something useful you overlooked.

2. Life is always unfolding as it must, regardless of your opinion.

There is an integrity to life, a wholeness that always includes everything, because life by its very nature works by certain immutable principles that are present in all of creation. Instead of fighting or withdrawing from life as it is, remind yourself that you're in the right place at the right time. The point of leverage is right where you are.

3. Everything works in relationship and nothing happens in isolation.

This is apparent when you look to the heavens and see the delicate balance of the stars and planets, or when you witness the majesty of the microcosmic workings of your own cells and organs, or discern the intricate interconnections of ecosystems within ecosystems that constitute the natural world. Whenever you feel cut off and apart from what is happening in your life, remind yourself that you are a part of what is happening. Then do your part to change it.

4. You are a unique and necessary part of the design of life.

The circumstances of your birth and development, the combination of your teachers and parents and peers, your mistakes and successes all add up to a one of a kind that cannot be duplicated. The world would be a lesser place without you. You are a unique inventory of experience, so take your inventory off the shelf. Put it to good use and connect yourself to the greater scheme of things.

5. You are the source of what you experience.

While you may not be the author of all circumstance, you are constantly authoring your perceptions, your actions, and your perceptions of the reactions to your actions. If you're unhappy with the play, rewrite the script.

6. You will always prove yourself right.

Whether you think you're right or your wrong, whether you blame your circumstances or take responsibility for your circumstances, you will work with great diligence to find evidence of what you assume to be true in order to prove yourself right. Whether it makes you happy or miserable, angry or curious, you succeed at being right. Choose carefully what you want to be right about.

7. As part of the design of life, you can observe nature's laws in yourself.

You have the ability to pay attention to your own life and, over time, discern the principles by which your life works. This is what differentiates human beings from every other living thing on earth. We are self-aware, and able to observe and learn, and refine our learning. There are no failures except the failure to learn. Make your own experiences your best teacher.

8. You have leverage to make tomorrow different than yesterday.

Those who fail to learn the lessons of history may be doomed to repeat them, but you are not limited by yesterday. The past has no control over your future. Use this moment to engage in breakthrough thinking about the future, and set in motion the events of a new tomorrow.

9. Defining a direction creates momentum for change.

It is given to each of us in life to oppose what we don't like, withdraw from what we cannot stand, or aim for what we want instead. If all you know is what you don't want, you will get more of it. Take aim and move forward.

10. Almost anything is possible.

They said "if man was meant to fly, he would have had wings." So he invented wings and learned to fly. You only limit is your imagination, so why limit yourself? In a world where technological breakthroughs and miracles of faith have become commonplace, lines of limitations eliminate possibilities. Erase the limiting line, and a whole world of options opens before you.

As you make wise choices in a mixed world, you can have a life by design.

INVENTORY YOUR EXPERIENCE: POST'EM WHERE YOU'LL SEE'EM

Pick the assumptions from this chapter that you want to own for yourself. Right them down and post them in a place where you will see them each day.

Add to the list with other useful assumptions. Each day your are cultivating a healthy attitude.

Part 4

MAKING CHOICES
ABOUT RELATIONSHIPS

We must learn to live together...or perish together as fools.
— Martin Luther King, Jr.

18. CONNECTING WITH YOURSELF

IT'S ABOUT TIME

*Life moves pretty fast. You don't stop and
look around, you could miss it.*
- Ferris Buehler's Day Off

Got a minute? We'll try to keep this brief. Everyone of us shares the mandate of getting more done in less time. You can just feel the time pressure when you listen to how people talk about time. Time to get moving. Time waits for no one. Always running out of time. There's never enough time. Pressed for time. Time waits for no one. Time flies when you're having fun.

Wouldn't it be terrific if you could take what spare time you have, and put it in a daylight savings account? Or at least in a 'Time Share'? Then, whenever you needed a little extra time, you could go get some! But it doesn't work that way. And while almost everyone has time to spare, most don't spare the time to create a life by design, to find happiness in their pursuits. Instead, they use their spare time to forget their unhappiness, distracting themselves into mindless and meaningless activities that contribute nothing but the killing of time. For those who have no time to spare for truly living, life becomes a relentless cycle of eat, work, eat, work, eat, watch TV, sleep, start again.

We're calling time out! After all, what could be more important than taking the time to exercise your freedom to live your life by design? The truth about time is that there is no better time than the present, and this is that moment. All other moments are in the dead past and the imagined future! When you started reading this it was now. Now it is now. And when you finish reading this and move on to something else, it will still be now. You live, eat, breathe, sleep, and perform all your basic functions now and only now! You've got to become a good friend of now if you want to know what it is to be a human being. To be more fully human, you've got to spend more time in this moment. That is why you are called a human being instead of a human doing!

Because the reality of life is happening only in this moment, there's only so much you can fit into now, only so much you can do and only so much you can pay attention to! Considering that your past is nothing more then the sum total of the choices you made in your now moments, if you now begin filling your now moments with thoughts, words, feelings, and actions that are dear and important to you, then when you look back on the dead past from your imagined future, you'll find that it, too, has been filled with fulfillment!

On the other hand, if you miss out on this moment by distracting yourself with thoughts, words, feelings and actions that aren't really important to you, then when you look back on the dead past from your imagined future, you will find it unfulfilling, because it's filled with failure and regret! Considering that there are no guarantees of anything you desire ever coming to pass, the only moment in which happiness is even a possibility is this one! That means, if you want to be happy, you've got to learn to be happy with life as it is, right now.
180

WHAT IS AND WHAT AIN'T

Though we travel the world over to find the beautiful,
we must carry it with us or we find it not.
- Ralph Waldo Emerson

What pulls people out of this moment? At least two time destroyers quickly come to mind: Comparisons of how life is to how life isn't, and un-experience when it comes to having time for more of the present in your life.

Whenever you compare what you have to what you don't have, and decide that what you don't have means everything while what you do have means nothing, you cease to be here now. We're not saying that you will necessarily disappear from anyone else's experience. But you will disappear from your own. Remember, this is it, and right now is the only moment in which you can experience fulfillment.

Here's a little trick to help you let go of what isn't real. The next time you find yourself making the comparison where now is worth less than something that isn't happening, pick up anything unbreakable and drop it a few times. Have different opinions about doing this each time you drop it, like "What a waste of my time." Pick it up again and drop it. "This is silly." Drop. "It's not fair!" Drop. And as soon as you notice that none of your opinions have any influence whatsoever on the fact that you are picking it up and dropping it, pick it up and drop it one more time. Only this time, say "Oh well!" Then put the object away and get on with your life as it is!

UNEXPERIENCES

Adopt the pace of nature: her secret is patience.
- Ralph Waldo Emerson

Have you ever been on your way somewhere in your car, and you weren't really in a hurry, yet your foot got heavier and heavier on the gas pedal till' you were really pushing the limit (and perhaps exceeding it by several miles per hour?) Suddenly, someone jumps lanes and gets in front of you, and you find yourself irritated with them for slowing you down when you weren't in a hurry to begin with? This is an example of having an "un- experience." It means that you've projected yourself forward to a place you are not, thus failing to be in the place that you are. The problem with "unexperiences" is that you become a danger to yourself and those around you by attempting to occupy space and time that isn't here yet!

These problems are easily remedied. Here are a few quick suggestions:

You better slow down

When you're not in a hurry, drive a little more slowly than the speed limit. This is especially important for you if you frequently find yourself exceeding the speed limit and then getting frustrated with the person in front of you who refuses to do the same! In a way, those people slowing you down are doing you a favor, because if you're not here now while driving a car, there's a very good chance that both you and the people around you are in danger from your driving behavior. However, if you're one of those people who always goes more slowly than you have to, the preceding advice doesn't really apply to you. In fact, you might want to hurry it up a little, since you're frustrating the heck out of the rest of us!

Let the Phone Enjoy Ringing

Wait a moment before answering it. We know people that, upon the sound of the ringing phone, drop whatever they're doing, rally their entire nervous system to get to the phone immediately. You'd think it was a fire alarm! A compulsion to answer the phone is a signal that you're not here right now. Relax, people will leave their name and number at the tone, or they'll still be talking to your machine when you pick it up to say hello. Instead of rushing to answer the phone, let the ringing of the phone first remind you to breathe and relax, to catch up to yourself before trying to get caught up with the person on the line.

Bathe More Often

No kidding! Life stinks when you bring home all the stress of work and attempt to share your sullied present with your loved ones. If it makes sense for you to start your day fresh when going to work, doesn't it also make sense to start your day fresh when coming home? Take a shower, a bath, or a quick sponge bath, and wash away the day's activities. Then slip into something a little more comfortable, and be a comfortable person for others to live with.

Meals: The Pause That Refreshes

The root word for nourishment means 'to cherish.' Before eating anything, stop! Breathe. Appreciate what you're about to consume, or appreciate that you're about to eat, or appreciate that you have a choice about what, when, where and how you eat. Some people have a habit of having a moment of grace before meals, and if that's your practice, then more power to you. Yet even the habitual saying of grace is no guarantee that you're creating a receptive space in your system for the vitamins, minerals, fiber, protein, water and fat that you're about to introduce into it. To make the most out of meals, make the most out of the moment in which you consume them.

These things will increase your sense of the present moment, and help you discover the time so you can take the time for a life by design.

GIVING YOURSELF A BREAK

There is more to life than increasing in speed
- Gandhi

You can eat right, and exercise regularly. But to gain the full benefits of diet and exercise, you must also learn to relax. All work and no relaxation dulls the mind, dulls the sense, interferes with creative thought, undermines your best intentions and leads to self-destructive habits. Relaxation is a key component of a life by design, because it frees you from stress and increases the likelihood that you will make wise choices in other areas of your life. And a state of relaxation is best achieved by taking the time to do things that you enjoy every day, and remembering to give yourself a break.

Yes, give yourself a break or you'll be on a path to burnout. The basic rule of life is that for every loss you suffer, you must replenish your supply. There's a science to it, because different kinds of activities require different kinds of breaks!

For starters, there's a simple relaxation technique that you can use almost any time, and any place where you're feeling a bit tense and irritable. Starting with your toes, progressively contract all the muscles in your feet, then let go, while breathing in and out in a slow and gentle manner. Next contract and release the muscles in your legs, then slowly work your way up to your buttocks, back, torso, shoulders, arms, fingers, and finally your face. You'll be amazed at the renewed sense of focus this can give you. Of course the expression on your face may need to be explained to anyone who happens to be a witness!

For example, if you have been sitting still, hunched over or glued to the phone, every 50 minutes or so, stand and stretch, walk down the hall or up a flight of stairs and get your circulation going again. You might even grab a jump rope and step outside for a few minutes of invigorating exercise. If you've been staring at figures or reading documents, an effective way to recharge is to stop and look out the window. Allow your eyes to relax, and let yourself see patterns in the clouds. Or, close your eyes, and imagine being in your favorite place of beauty, and do a quick systems check of your five senses to see how much of that place you can bring into the moment: Sight, sounds, smells, tastes, along with feelings and sensations. Filling your senses

184

with life is a great way to revive yourself when you've been swimming in the details too long!

If your work requires lots of concentration and accuracy, you can switch to something playful for a few minutes in order to change your internal state. Read the comics, juggle, play with a windup toy, draw a picture with crayons or play a mindless game on the computer. This would probably not be the time for Doom™, Abuse™, or Descent™ into hellish scenarios of blood and destruction! If you must, use those computer games to discharge your stress after dealing with a difficult person or situation.   When you've been hard at work on a task that requires creative thinking, switch to filing, or unpacking a briefcase, or any other task that is mindless, mechanical, and clears your work space.

Get how this works? Whatever you've been doing, do the opposite! If you've been working alone for many hours, interact with someone else. Talking, laughing, and responding to other people's reactions can be a real energy lift. And if you've been in meetings all days, take ten minutes for yourself.   We hope you're not getting the idea that working is how you take a break from all those breaks you've been taking.   But if your cup is empty, there's nothing left in it for living your life by design! We think it's reasonable to recharge your system a few times a day, even if only for a minute or two.

LEARNING TO LET GO

Within you there is a stillness and sanctuary to which
you can retreat at anytime and be yourself.
- Hermann Hesse

Here is one last time prescription for you.   It requires nothing of you except time, and is scientifically guaranteed to change your life for the better. Your memory will improve, your concentration will improve, your blood pressure may go down, and the aging process will slow down. Are you interested? We're about to make a big deal out of nothing, because all you have to do is nothing for ten to twenty minutes a day. Maybe you're now thinking that you're way ahead on this one, so allow us to explain what we mean by nothing. Not planning, not dreaming, not thinking and not sleeping, doing nothing refers to just sitting quietly and doing the one thing necessary to keeping you alive right now. That's breathing, in and out, and then in again.

First, the research: One study on this kind of relaxation program related to job satisfaction. After eleven months of sitting quietly for 20 minutes a day, most people showed a 75% increase in job satisfaction. Another study related to the effect of a continued relaxation program on alcohol and cigarette consumption showed a 50% reduction in both habits within 10 months. Perhaps this gentle improvement was the result of providing an alternative that fulfilled the intent often hidden behind smoking and drinking of reducing stress. Once that intent is fulfilled, the alcohol and cigarette consumption naturally begins to fall away.

What would you give to slow down the aging process? Because it turns out that if you're willing to give 10 to 20 minutes a day of your life to nothing (except sitting and breathing), you can slow down your biological age (how well you function.) Of course, your chronological age (how old you are from the day you are born until now) will still be the same. But in a study that measured eyesight, hearing, blood pressure, and other parameters, those participants in the study who invested 20 minutes a day in doing nothing (except sitting and breathing) measured 2.2 years younger biologically than chronologically. After one month , they measured five years younger biologically. After three years, this same group of people measured twelve years younger biologically than chronologically. Their vision improved, their hearing improved, their blood pressure improved. They got physiologically younger, even though they were chronologically aging.

Some people find sitting and breathing to be a simple and pleasant (non-) activity. Others find that their minds race and their
186

thoughts pour through their mind in a never ending tumble. If you're one of the latter, here is a simple four part method for doing nothing! (Hey, don't laugh! Every little bit helps when learning to do something new that will benefit you the rest of your life!)

Comfortable Position

You want to sit or lay down in a comfortable position, one in which you are not likely to fall asleep. We find that sitting works best for people just beginning to learn this.

Quiet Environment

Find a place away from the maddening crowd. If no such place exists, then create a buffer around yourself with signs on the door reading 'Quiet: Genius Doing Nothing,' and if it helps, use some ear plugs or sound blocking headphones.

Focal Point

Breathing, as we've suggested, works as the perfect focal point, because it is always there. (If it isn't there, then frankly, you won't need this technique because you're already dead!) There are alternatives to breathing and you're welcome to experiment and find something that works best for you. For example, if there's a particular prayer that you find comforting, say it over and over again slowly, listening to the meaning of each word and phrase at a deeper and deeper level. Or, you can use some mental image that you find relaxing, like a mountain meadow, or a beach with lapping waters. You may want to add a sound to the mix, such as hearing the waves coming in and going out with each breath, or a word that evokes calm in you like 'peace' or 'easy' that you repeat over and over with each breath. Or just pay attention to the rise and fall of your breathing. Breathe in slowly on the inhale, then at the top of the breath, let go. As soon as you reach the bottom of your breath, start breathing in again. Emphasize the inspiration, as the exhale can take care of itself.

Passive Attitude

A passive attitude is one where nothing is required of you. This means that if you find your mind racing a few minutes later, you accept it and go back to your breathing. If you find that you dozed off for a moment, you accept it and go back to your breathing. If you hear a car door slam, a doorbell ring, or a dog bark, you notice it and then go back to your breathing.

Here is how this will benefit you. Each day that you do this, your body/mind will let go of a little stress. Less stress will allow you to get more satisfaction out of the rest of your day, have clear communications with the people you care about, and make healthier choices. But that's only the beginning of the benefits. Every day that you lower your resistance to life as it is, you increase the resistance of your immune system by giving more power to life support and less power to the shields. Learning to do nothing when there's nothing happening is a first step towards learning how to relax in the midst of a crisis, so that you can have clearer thoughts and better ideas on how to navigate through the storm.

But wait, there's more! This little (non)activity can enhance the clarity you bring to setting your goals! Just do nothing first, and then begin to brainstorm your goals, and you'll find that they have less to do with today's issues and more to do with the quality of your life. This is also a great way to set the stage for accessing resources and associating them to a particular project. Just do nothing first (except breathe and relax) and you'll find yourself gaining new insights into seemingly intractable problems.

INVENTORY YOUR EXPERIENCE: ACROSS THE UNIVERSE

Drop And Give Us Ten.   If you haven't done so yet, take ten minutes now to breathe and do nothing.   Learn firsthand the 'more with less' power of nothing to change everything.   Then pick an optimal time to do this each day, so that you can develop a habit that will be with you in the present, as you consider the dead past, and as you look ahead to the imagined future.

After you've completed these activities, then join us in the next part of the book, where we'll explore the connections between your life by design, the quality of your closest relationships, and how the world turns out.

19. BUILDING BRIDGES

YOU ARE NOT ALONE

*Every carbon atom in your body has been in a star,
been blown out, gone into a cloud and been reformed
into another star about five times, before it ended up
on earth and in you.*
-Tony Stark, Astronomer

As dads and as doctors, we've had the opportunity to assist home
births and help bring new life into the world. It isn't unusual in
home birth situations for the new dad to want to catch his child in
that first moment of birth. To do so, he must open his hands wide
in order to receive this delicate new life. We've noticed that many of
the babies born into loving homes sleep with their hands completely
open, relaxed, delicately resting on the sheets and blankets. Some
babies come into the world kicking and screaming, and when they
sleep, their little hands become fists clenched tight, as if resisting the
world. The ancient Chinese believed in a connection between the
hands and heart.

Years ago, in a fund raiser called Hands Across America, people joined hands, from the west coast to the east coast. Images of this event were on TV, in the magazines and newspapers. What made it remarkable was the amount of interest and cooperation that it produced! They stood together all the way across the vast land mass of the United States with their hands open; open to life; open to each other; open to a united state of participation and belonging.

When it comes to charity, most people would rather open their hands to give than receive. For a person in trouble financially or emotionally, the most difficult thing is to admit the need, and open up to receiving help. People going through severe down cycles seem certain that 'giving is good, taking is bad.' Yet the reality of life is that there are no givers without takers! Every person on the receiving end makes it possible for everyone on the giving end to be a contributor. People in need are giving the givers the opportunity to make a difference! Consider the symmetry of that, and you can see yet again how everything works together!

WHEN DO YOU CLOSE YOUR HANDS?

Do not protect yourself by a fence,
but rather by your loved ones.
-Czech Proverb

Not surprisingly, when people are angry their hands become fists. And as they do, their jaw tightens, their breathing tightens, and their blood pressure goes up as they close down their connection to the world around them. But it isn't just anger that causes the hands to close and the heart to grow heavy.

A single dad, trying to raise his small child, found himself suddenly out of work, then out of money. When he lost his home and car, he ran out of self-respect. A caring person heard of his plight, and offered a room underneath her house with a table, a chair, a single bed, a hotplate and a small refrigerator. "It's not much," she told him, "but it's at least it's something while you get back on your feet." The little room became their home during the winter months when no work could be found. The father tried to hide his worries from his child during the daylight hours. Each night he waited until she had fallen asleep, then sat in the chair and tried to figure a way out of their impoverished situation.

'Twas the night before Christmas, and all through the room, no one was stirring in the light of the moon. He sat at the table feeling sorry for himself, and sorrier for his child. As he cursed his luck, and felt the heavy burden of being unable to provide for someone he loved so deeply, the damn burst, and he began to sob uncontrollably from all that pent up misery and sadness. This woke the child, who sat up and said, "You know, Daddy, we sure are lucky. We have a roof over our heads, food in our bellies, and we have each other. Everything will be okay. Get some rest." Her hands were open, her heart was open, and she was able to receive the small good available and be nourished by it. In his child's example, he found himself again.

FIND YOUR ALLIES

Wherever I have wandered, a path has appeared.
I have been helped, supported, encouraged
and nurtured by people.
I have, to the best of my ability, returned help,
support, encouragement and nurture.
- Alice Walker, 'In Search Of Our Mother's Gardens'

When do you close your hands? When do you allow yourself to become isolated, to think you live outside of the common universe, alone, alienated, a stranger in a strange land? Isolation is the deadliest disease of all. Your ability to give of yourself will evaporate if you allow yourself to become empty and alone. To give, you must first receive. To receive, you must be willing for others to give to you, to nourish you, to support you. There is no giving without receiving; there is no receiving without giving. It goes hand in hand, just like breathing in and breathing out. To truly live, to thrive, to be fully alive, you have to do both, not one or the other. Sometimes the greatest contribution you can make is giving someone your willingness to receive. Giving does NOT make someone a better person, but it does put us into the flow of the energy of life.

When your hands are closed, you must be holding on to something! Whatever grudges you carry and fears you cling to become walls that separate you from the support and nourishment of others. Yet you can let go of whatever you're holding onto - if you want to remove the barriers. You have to breathe in, inspire yourself and let go.

You don't need to be in a crisis to connect yourself to others. You are never alone if you're willing to reach out for the support that is there. Take every opportunity to build bridges between yourself and the people around you, and find your allies. Do you have friends with whom you can share your concerns and deepest feelings? People you can depend on? Do you have sources of honest feedback? Do you have good sources for high quality information? Do you have advocates who will speak out on your behalf? Do you have associates who are will to challenge you? Rather than depending on one or two people to play all of these support roles for you, you can cultivate an abundance of relationships that support you in these ways and more.

OUNCES OF PREVENTION

When you make a world tolerable for yourself,
you make a world tolerable for others.
- Anais Nin

While you're never alone and you do have allies, keeping those allies requires that you regularly build bridges and destroy walls. Here are six ounces of prevention that are worth tons of cure when it comes to a support system that works. Kids, try this at home. And try this with your kids!

Give Appreciation

You can pull weeds or you can plant flowers. And you can plant so many flowers that the weeds have no place to grow. A study done at the University of Maryland to determine what motivates people to give of themselves at work revealed that appreciation is first on the list. In family systems, the same holds true. When you give appreciation to the people you care about, you cause a wave of good energy that adds prevents problems and washes away much conflict. "Thanks for being honest." "Thanks for taking the time." "Hey, thanks for making this house look so beautiful." "Thanks for being out there earning a living for us." "Thank you for taking care of the children." "Thank you for being a wonderful child." "Thank you for cleaning up your room." "Thank you for bringing this to my attention." "Thank you for saying 'Thank you.'" You're welcome! It's great to get the whole family involved in acknowledging and appreciating each other. It just begins to build this swell of good energy, and before you know it, the problems start to dissolve; they are really put into perspective.

Identify the Positive Intent

Intent is the purpose behind behavior, and that includes the behavior of communication. Wouldn't it be wonderful if our good intentions were recognized and appreciated even when our efforts failed? But instead, as we say in our book 'Dealing With People You Can't Stand,' the road to hell is paved with good intentions. Have you ever meant well, and someone took it the wrong way? Do you know how awful that feels? Then you know that good intentions are clearly not enough.

You know how it goes. Instead of saying "I care about you and I want to clear the air about something that's in the way of my positive feelings about you," somebody says "You really upset me when you said..." That's as far as they get before the other person, who now feels under attack, becomes defensive, and a raging argument ensues.

However, you can get better mileage out of your good intentions. Just tell people your positive intent when you tell them about your concerns or about your feelings. That's a great way to turn an argument into connection and creative thinking, because people need to know where you are coming from in order to respond appropriately.

You can flip this around too! After all, you can't depend on other people to communicate clearly. Yet you can look for the positive intent of others, and realize that a nagging mother is expressing her love, that a pushy coworker is racing against a (possibly self-imposed) deadline, or that a wishy washy response from a child is a way of avoiding the ugliness of conflict. If the nagging mother complains about the way you are dressed, you can say "Thanks for caring about my appearance." If the pushy coworker is intense about a deadline, you can say "Thanks for wanting to move this forward." And with the wishy washy child, you can soften your tone, and say "Thanks for reminding me to calm myself down."

Listen To Understand

To have an argument, two people must want to be understood simultaneously, and neither person wants to understand. The truth be told, it is a waste of your time trying to be understood by someone who wants to be understood. Instead, understand the other person first, and make sure that they know it. Give people feedback that you're listening, whether it's a nod of the head a meaningful look, or an occasional grunt. Do you know why people repeat themselves? Do you know why? Do you? People repeat themselves because they want feedback that they've been heard. Whenever you feed back what you've heard, you let people know that you're listening. Whenever you listen first and ask questions later, you demonstrate that you want to understand. And when you put listening and then asking questions together, people feel understood.

Behavioral Definitions

How do you show someone that you care? People define the same experiences in different ways, and define different experiences in the same way. Justin and Casey were good friends with a little problem in problem solving. If either of them was upset, the other would consistently make it worse. Yet how was this possible? They were both trying to help! To understand why it wasn't working for either of them, consider their two ways of defining how friends 'should' treat upset friends. When Justin is upset, he thinks that a good friend 'should' become interested and ask a lot of questions. When Casey is upset, he thinks that a good friend 'should' leave him alone to work it out. What happens when they do unto one another? Casey leaves Justin alone and Justin feels abandoned. Justin pesters Casey with questions and Casey feels annoyed. Nobody gets what they want, and everybody gets more upset. Yet their problem could be easily solved if only they knew each other's complex of equivalents for friendship when either is upset. Then, Casey would know to ask Justin questions, and Justin would know to leave Casey alone.

The golden rule tells us to "Do unto others as you would have them do unto you," and that's great advice. But to do it in a way that another person understands, find out their complex of equivalents. When someone tells you you're not doing something, and you know that you are, ask, "How would you know if I was?" Someone says "You don't care!" And you reply, " How would you know if I cared?" Someone tells you "You're not listening to me!" You reply " How would you know if I was listening?" But you don't need to wait until someone accuses you falsely to find out their complex of equivalents. Instead, be proactive, and ask what the people in your life need to see and hear in order for them to know that you're caring, supportive, listening, and being a friend in a difficult moment. Then do yourself a favor and define these terms for you, so you'll know what to ask for when you need the assistance of others.

Communication agreements

We live in a world of mostly invisible social agreements that govern all of our relationships in the vast realm of relationship bordered by order and chaos. Over the years, these agreements get refined and redefined, yet they are always present, and mostly invisible. You can make the invisible visible by invoking these agreements and putting them in writing: agreements about communication, finance, problem solving, everything.

Rick and Rick aren't just business partners in book and tape projects. We are the best of friends. In many ways, we're better friends now than in the beginning of our partnership. We had the occasional conflict in the early days of our business. Conflict? Sometimes it seemed like all out war. As partners in practice and co-presenters in workshops, we regularly misunderstood each other and disagreed about who ought to do what, when, where and how. But we grew tired of the struggle, and hit upon the idea of coming to agreement. We drafted a document, and called it 'Com-Strat,' which is Starfleet language for 'communication strategy.' We made it a point to have our document of agreements on a table or on the wall at every business meeting. If either of us strayed from the agreements, the other just pointed at them and we were back on track. Within six months, the on-paper version had become unnecessary. Friends and partners for over 20 years, we no longer argue with each other because effective communication with each other has become our habit. Maybe it will become yours, too!

Here are a few such communication agreements, taken from our files. They were worked out in counseling by couples and families choosing to live their lives by design, and in training sessions by self-managed teams wanting to cut their losses and be more productive. Some are general ground rules that must be defined for all parties. Others are specific communication actions that need no further definition. We offer these as examples, and encourage you to develop your own.'

- Whoever spoke first, goes first.

- We do not change the subject until the subject is understood.

- We let each other know we're listening by backtracking.

- When sharing ideas, we share the thoughts behind them.

- We ask for what we want.

- We respect our differences in interests and opinions.

- We share equal responsibility for solving our problems.

- We strive for cooperation over coercion

- We desire to learn from each other rather than defending ourselves.

- We speak our intent, and look for positive intent in each other.

- We take the time to co-develop our vision of the future

- We accept change in each other.

Exit From Stupidity Strategies

Ever notice that period of discomfort that follows an uncomfortable interaction, that moment of recognition that you or the other person has behaved badly and knows it? When you know you did something stupid and someone is upset with you as a result, that's a good time for an exit strategy. Not an exit from the room or an exit from the relationship, but an exit from continuing the stupidity! Every relationship is unique (wife/husband, parent/child, manager/employee), and exit strategies are unique to every relationship. Exit strategies save a lot of time, help you to leave the past behind quickly, and get back on track with a life by design.

Gary Kirschner may vex his wife Evelyn to the point of aggravation. But when he asks for understanding by loudly proclaiming 'Hey, I've got to live with me too, you know,' she has to laugh. When we Ricks get annoyed with each other, we exaggerate our problem to lighten things up. This doesn't work as well with our wives, who may not be amused. Lindea K prefers a simple admission of guilt, while Lisa B prefers an honest apology. A friend of ours, while laughing like an idiot, responds to her room-mate's anger by throwing her hands up in the air and repeating the words 'Mea Culpa' over and over again until they're both laughing! A business acquaintance jokes about his own ineptitude whenever he lets down a customer, while another summarizes what has happened and says the best thing she can think of to put it in perspective. This is clearly a case of different strokes for different folks, but there's no reason to continue down the road of stupidity when you can take the next on ramp to the highway.

INVENTORY YOUR EXPERIENCE: DRAW BRIDGES

See The Support. Here's your chance to design a diverse support system that can help you live your life by design. If you find that you

don't have the suggested number of people in a particular role, you can make it a goal sheet in your planner.

1. Friends. People who you can have fun with, but who will also listen when you need to ventilate your exhaust or talk about your concerns. List five of your closest friends, and how their friendship supports you in life.

2. Associates. People with whom you can share information and ideas related to shared interests at work or in the community. Name four people who support you in this way.

3. Role Models. People who inspire you by the example they set, who could deal with your problems in an admirable way. Living or dead, identify your top three role models, and describe what you most admire about them.

4. Mentors. People who have traveled the road you're on, who have been there, done that, and bought the t-shirt, and can show you the way. Identify at least one person who can play this role in your life.

5. Teachers. People who can help you improve your skill in specific areas. Identify at least one teacher in your life, and the skill they're helping you to develop or improve.

6. Guardian Angels. People who can help you by using their influence and contacts to help you along your way. Name at least one individual who looks out for you like this.

When you've completed drawing these bridges of support, join us in the next chapter, where we'll take an intimate look at keeping love alive.

20. LOVING FOR LIFE

LIKE WATER, LIKE CHOCOLATE

In your eyes, the light, the heat. In your eyes, I am complete. In your eyes, the resolution of all the fruitless searches.
- Peter Gabriel

There is a sweetness in life that can only be known through a loving and committed relationship. A unique joy is revealed when two souls join together to form a union, built on purpose, support, encouragement, communication, companionship and shared pleasure. Relationships accelerate your awareness of yourself, and in this way they enhance your aliveness while easing the sense of isolation that begins at birth.

Yet relationships have their seasons, from the passion of youth to the maturity of old age, with mid-life crises, and menopause along the way. Sometimes the changing seasons can be bitterly difficult, challenging the most fundamental concepts each partner holds to be true about life, liberty and happiness. Loving relationships require hard work to make them work. Indeed, they are no refuge for the meek and the needy, because clarity and courage are the essential ingredients of a successful union. But for those who are willing to make and then honor the commitment, the reward of true love is one of the finest gifts life has to offer us.

THE SONG OF LOVE

To love another is to see the face of God
from the play 'Les Miserables'

True love between two committed people is such a compelling and grand mystery that throughout history, all sorts of comparisons to other experiences have been made in order to know the truth of love. Allow us to mix a few metaphors of our own.

Love is a song wanting to be sung, a song that harmonizes two lives into one. Harmony is an achievable state of serenity and synergy in which the energy flows and each one knows how to resonate with the other. Without harmony, all that is left is a din of discord. Fail to attend to the need for harmony, and you'll have to face the music. And that's where perfect practice makes perfect. Moments of audition and rehearsal present themselves daily, and through time, patience and work, they become memorable moments of transcendence and delight.

Navigate the treacherous shores carefully, and you may find that love is a safe harbor from the turmoil of a mixed up world. No longer ships passing in the night or adrift in an ocean of emotion, true love provides you with the opportunity to safely experience the worst and best of you, to hold steady as you find the sea-bottom with the anchor of your commitment, to view each other against the starry skies of your hopes and dreams, your faces illuminated by your hearts.

Love is a garden of hopes and dreams. This garden must be

watered and fertilized with loving attention for it to become an Eden. Without attention, the weeds of stress will take over and decrease the love produced in both quantity and quality. This garden must be weeded and pruned with understanding and forgiveness. When lovers tend to this garden, they make their home in paradise.

These are just a few of the metaphors people use to describe their experience of the mystery and truth of love.

The reality of love is that it takes a lot of work to make it work. Why? Consider what you're dealing with! While people remain recognizable as themselves throughout their lifetime, it is the nature of every person to be changing constantly. Add two such changing creatures together, and it's obvious that a couple in relationship is at least as complicated as the parts. Add the fast pace of change to this basic complexity of humans in love, and the odds are that you and your beloved will be out of sorts with each other at least some of the time. If it happens enough of the time, the loving nature of this most important relationship can be transformed into memory upon memory of hurt, anger, hassle and boredom.

The romantic notion that love just happens and then sustains itself is a pleasant fantasy that bears little resemblance to the way life actually works. No healthy relationship is devoid of pain and dysfunction. But when the pain is greatest, for love to last, you must recognize it as an opportunity to deepen your capacity for love.

RELATING TO STRESS
It is very difficult to maintain a relationship based solely on mistrust.
-Pierce Brosnan as Remington Steele

Sadly, many couples allow their relationships to become so stress-filled that, in the end, all that's left for the couple is their relationship to stress rather than to the love that brought them together in the first place. Since stress leads to exhaustion and exhaustion leads to death, the idea of being together 'till death do we part' has certainly earned its place in the marriage ceremony.

Stress has many awful expressions, first and foremost of which is projection. A natural consequence of living together over time is an increasing sensitivity to each other's habits. Those behaviors you dislike most in your partner are often ones you have yourself, though you're likely to be oblivious to this. One person yells "You're not listening to me" while refusing to listen to the other. "You only think of yourself!" while thinking only of their own needs and feelings. By projecting these bad feelings about yourself onto your partner, you can hold yourself blameless and still have someone to blame!

Another common form of relationship stress is dependency, where partners come to view each other as children, because they act like children, needing to be cared for rather than cared about. Stress can also cause passive and aggressive tendencies tend to be expressed in relationships, so that instead of moving towards one another, couples move against or away from one another. While there are physical causes of sexual dysfunction and disinterest, it can also be the inevitable result of collected guilt, anxiety, anger and disapproval.

Whatever form the stress takes, couples learn all sorts of ways to adapt to it. Some let an argument cook on the back burner until the heat builds up enough to make the relationship unbearable and somebody has to leave. Others turn the heat all the way up, bringing the subject to a boil with their angry words and actions. Over time, all it takes is a flicker of an eyelash and war erupts in the kitchen. Then there are those couples who avoid confrontation at all costs. While it may seem the most civilized adaptation, it is has an explosive potential that for some couples makes it the most dangerous of all. Or the relationship may simply rot out from beneath them both, and then suddenly collapse.

FIXING WHAT ISN'T BROKEN

We are shaped and fashioned by what we love.
- Goethe

A funny thing happens on the way to a relationship. You're drawn to someone like yourself in many ways, maybe someone who laughs at the same things, comes from a similar background, or has some of the same goals and dreams and fears. But on this common ground, couples may get trapped in a denial of their differences, as if being different is somehow a detriment. Yet differences can be complementary. Typically, what one partner lacks, the other has in abundance. Differences can be a relationship fulfilling asset, when both parties see the value of them!

Many people have the mistaken idea that their purpose in a relationship is to fix their partner. In fact, the opposite is true, because in a healthy and happy relationship, you learn more about yourself than you ever could about your partner. And no matter how many years you have together, your partner will always be somewhat of a mystery to you. In this regard, relationships offer an interesting mirror in a hall of mirrors.

For example, when one person says 'Quit trying to change me!" they are demanding that the other person change! Is it not an attempt to discourage your partner when you say "Why do you try to so hard to discourage me?!" Whenever a relationship slides into a conflict of rightness about the wrongness of each other, frustration can only build. Each side finds proof of the defects of the other, until all that remains is flaws and failings. And so each in their own way gets caught up in battling with the mirrored and mirroring image of self, and forgets who it was that needed the repair.

Yet what is it that needs to be fixed? For starters, those fixated perceptions you project onto each other! A powerful truth of loving relationship is that couples first engage with each other because of shared values plus interesting differences. It makes no sense to eliminate those very differences you first found appealing, when instead they could be enjoyed, cherished, and encouraged! More often than not, it is a terrible mistake to think of your partner as flawed, no matter how flawed he or she appears to be. For whatever you dislike in one another, is quite likely to be something you dislike more in yourself.

SUFFERING FROM NEGLECT

See me. Feel me. Touch me. Heal me.
- from 'Tommy' the rock opera

The flip side of the fight response is the flight response, in the form of neglect. That's when walking away or avoiding 'certain subjects' becomes the dominant relationship strategy. Soon, the relationship comes to resemble more a boarding house than a loving home. Avoidance of your partner is a way of giving up the battle without losing the war. But it is also a kind of cowardice that must, through time, create a deepening fissure between you.

Of course, not all neglect is a flight response. Sometimes, it represents a loss of interest due to changing goals. We recall one husband who had approached falling in love and getting married as a goal to be achieved rather than a value to be fulfilled. The end result was that once he had accomplished his goal, he redirected the now available energy to other goals, neglecting his new wife in the process. Many people have such foolish concepts, believing that when love comes along, it comes to stay, that relationships can sustain themselves and run on automatic once they get going .

Another cause of neglect is the mistaken idea that your partner's purpose in the relationship is to help you out professionally, creatively, socially or economically, to somehow complete your life without interfering with it. Yet it is the nature of life that when two people come together, each will temper and influence the other to some degree, and that if the relationship is to grow, there must occasionally be personal sacrifice for the good of the relationship as a whole. That doesn't mean both partners must lose as individuals in order to win as a couple, since committed relationships produce tremendous rewards that benefit both individuals as the result of the success of the relationship!

But perhaps the most common cause of neglect is that there seems to be too little energy left over, because both individuals have too much going on. First, the times we live in offer us a wide variety of opportunities for self expression and creative fulfillment, along with numerous responsibilities. Typically, both partners work and both partners also contribute at least some of their time to community activities, plus physical fitness needs, aging parents, and children who need attention too! Pulled in a seemingly infinite number of directions, the amount of energy spent pursuing them often exceeds the amount of energy produced in return.

The result is a deficit of energy available for love. And that leads to the cultivation of habits for managing, rather than making the most of, the time together. Get up. Go out. Come home. Have dinner. Watch TV. Go to bed. Get up. Too tired. Too busy. Too often, the language of love shows this neglect. Making love is the last thing on one or both of their minds, and there's the rub, or lack thereof. Failing to take the time to make love in a loving relationship leads to a slow starvation of the regenerative energy it produces, loving energy that is one of the greatest blessings and opportunities for deepening intimate relationships.

HOW TO MAKE YOUR HEARTS GROW FONDER
And in the end, the love you take is equal to the love you make.

-Lennon & McCartney

Now hear this: A relationship is both a workshop and a playground! Contrary to popular belief, absence is not the only way to make your hearts grow fonder. Next time conflict and unhappiness threaten to disrupt your commitment to living a life by design, here are a few simple methods for restoring love and harmony:

The 'Looking Thing.'

Have you ever gazed into the eyes of someone you loved, or thought you loved, and lost yourself there for a few minutes? That kind of feeling can be rekindled in relationships, no matter how cold or distant they've become. Like most things in life, it is a matter of will. If the eyes are the windows to the soul, sometimes instead of looking out, you might try letting someone look in. That is the basis of a wonderfully simple little exercise that couples can engage in, which we call the 'Looking Thing.' Here's how you do it: A couple gazes silently into each other's eyes for several uninterrupted minutes. That's it! We told you it was simple.

So simple in fact that most couples have never thought to do this in years, even though it was one of the forces that brought their relationship together in the first place. If you look into the eyes of your partner for more than a few moments, something changes in the way you see each other. Like breathing in and breathing out, you see and then you are seen, back and forth, as everything outside of your relationship falls away into the silence. At first, you may see either all that you love or everything you dislike about your partner, or some combination of the two. Then, you notice those eyes becoming more fluid, the face less defined. It's amazing when you stop and look , just how many people you can see there! At some point, the mental chatter stops, and a breakthrough occurs, and you both remember who you are instead of who you aren't. An incredible clarity comes through after only a few minutes of the "Looking Thing.' And when done regularly, the chemistry of love is renewed.

Play the Spoons

As a couple, you are an exercise in teamwork, hopefully growing in confidence that somebody has got you both covered. It's great to have someone with whom you can share your thoughts and dreams, fears and fantasies, and do projects like yard work and dishes. But the most precious sharing begins with the one thing that keeps you alive, your breathing. There is an activity that helps to bring renewal to a tired couple. Breathing together, like the looking thing, can renew your feelings of love and connection no matter how tired and distant you feel. This is even true in the midst of an argument. We call this activity 'Playing the spoons.' Here's how you do it.

Lay on your side, facing the same direction. One person hugs the other from behind. Can't decide who gets to be on the inside? Take turns! Close your eyes, and allow your breathing to synchronize. Don't force this, just allow it, because it is the natural direction your breathing wants to go. Focus on your heart and the heart of your beloved, until you experience the power of two becoming one. Or as one breathes out, the other can breathe in, and you can feel the energy flow between you.

Gifts of Love

What is that one thing your partner is always after you to do? Doing that is what we call a 'gift of love.' Guaranteed to be fulfilling to your partner, because they've told you that it is something they would love to receive from you! And guaranteed to be fulfilling to you when you're looking for just the right gift for a moment of appreciation.

The Truth Process

When distance replaces closeness and acting out replaces connecting up, that may be a sign that what needs to be said has been left unsaid. Just as cleaning the house is an important way to keep it livable, cleaning the lines of communication is an essential part of a happy relationship. The Truth Process is less about telling the truth, and more about inviting and then listening to it, less about expressing opinions and more about expressing feelings. Unlike non-intimate relationships (doctor-patient, lawyer-client, editor-writer, manager-worker, etc.), couples must take time to stay current with each other about their feelings, even though emotions are often illogical. The expression of feelings is not a request for help. Sharing feelings is an opportunity to give and receive support for self-reflection. Instead of exposing themselves to judgment, or being treated like they're broken, couples find it easier to understand their feelings when saying them out loud in a safe and encouraging environment.

Here's how it works. There can only be one transmitter at a time. Whoever has the most intense emotions gets to speak first. (Now, don't fight over this! Just look in each other's eyes, remember love, and you will see where the need is greatest!) When you're the receiver, listen like your life depends on it, listen for the truth, the whole truth, and nothing but the truth. Don't offer suggestions. Don't compare what you're hearing to your own experiences. Just say 'Tell me more!' until the only truth that remains is that nothing more needs to be said. At that point, you can wrap a hug around the truth process and feel the profound energy connection available to lovers who love enough to share what they care about.

If you're transmitting your truth, it is helpful to remember to speak from your own point of view, to communicate responsibly, to own your own stuff, to vent the exhaust instead of dumping it on the person you love most. However, sometimes you just need to talk, to get it out, to hear what you're saying and see what you feel. In that case, keep talking until the storm has passed. You can use the Truth Process whenever your relationship no longer makes sense! But telling the truth regularly keeps you current and connected through time.

Space, The Final Frontier

It's true: Absence really does make hearts grow fonder. Couples report that after retirement, or during the cabin fever of a long winter in a cold and rainy environment, they get on each other's nerves with greater frequency and intensity. The solution is a simple one. In an intimate relationship, each partner must cultivate some life of their own. Hobbies, projects, friendships and family offer opportunities for a little time apart when the walls are closing in. Taking space for time alone, time away, time to regain perspective, is an essential part of a happy and productive relationship.

INVENTORY YOUR EXPERIENCE: LOVE DANCE

Hopefully, this chapter has provided you with a few ounces of prevention worth tons of cure. If you're still looking for love and haven't yet found your partner for life, take what was useful and then please move on to the next chapter. However, if you are in a relationship and you're willing to have that relationship support your commitment to a life by design, there's no better time than the present to tell some truth.

Do The Truth Process. Once a week, for the next month, find a comfortable place to sit down facing one another, set aside a half hour to tell the truth. The topic: Whatever you've been afraid to discuss because it might bring up differences between you. You don't have to go for everything all at once. Start gently to build a safe environment for truth to be told. You may find that this works better when you take turns, or you may prefer to take your turns on different days completely. But in this process, remember not to interrupt, not to try to change anyone's mind , only to learn more and more about these feelings until there's nothing more to say except 'Thanks for listening with your heart.'

Then, hug, cuddle, or talk amongst yourselves before joining us in the next chapter to see the big picture of how your life by design determines how the world works out.

Part 5

CHOICES ABOUT THE WORLD

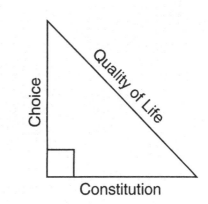

The future of humanity depends on the integrity of the individual. It is absolutely touch and go. Each one of us could make the difference.
-Buckminster Fuller

21. KNOWING THE WORLD

THE PARADIGM SHIFTS

Weep not that the world changes. Did it keep a sta-
ble changeless state, it were indeed cause to weep.
- William Cullen Bryant

Paradigms are sets of rules based on sets of assumptions about
how things work. As new tools lead to a better understanding of
nature's rules, humanity is witnessing and giving birth to a global
paradigm shift.   When the paradigm shifts, reality does not change,
it remains the same. All that changes is our perception of reality, and
as our perception changes, so do our actions. A paradigm shift is an
upgrade in perception and behavior, as our understanding of how
things actually work improves. But if the paradigm is shifting, what
is it shifting towards? To answer this question, we must first see what
we're shifting away from, and why.

The paradigm that we're leaving behind is an adversarial one, and
it defined humanity's social, cultural, political, religious and econom-
ic relations since the beginning of recorded history. It was based on

215

the idea that there is not enough good to go around, and that for someone to win, someone else must lose. This limited and limiting view of the world inevitably produced division, polarization and a narrowing of options for almost everyone in a relentless struggle for supremacy. Since every problem needed a win/lose solution, the consequence was to expend great amounts of energy and resources that at best created compromises that didn't really work for either side of the issue in question. At worst, a state of gridlock and non-action prevailed.

Polarized and adversarial people see life in ones and zeros, when in truth a wide range of choices is available in almost every situation. Adversaries develop labeling systems that make it easy to know who must lose in order for someone to win (liberal/conservative; pro-life/pro-choice; black/white, Arab/Jew, catholic/protestant, east/west). Yet such labels typically leave out the shades of gray that would add contrast and depth to our ability to solve problems in meaningful and productive ways. While all sides of a divisive issue may have something to contribute to its resolution, in the old paradigm, those contributions could not be made. They fell beyond the range of acceptability for those who stood to gain the most from a house divided.

Divide and conquer is a well known principle to those who crave power and control over others. Many so-called leaders in government and industry today continue to promote an adversarial paradigm when it suits their purpose. They know that fear (of losing) and anger (at having lost) are useful leverage points for promoting polarization. Using this simple and time-tested trick, they succeed at getting people to distance themselves from each other because of small differences instead of building the bridges on which the future depends. Sadly, it has often been easier to go along with such foolishness or remain silent about it, rather than run the risk of finding oneself on the bleeding edge of change.

Another destructive element of the old paradigm was the belief that humanity is somehow separate from the environment, that it is our destiny to conquer the earth, dominate it and exploit it at will.

While this has been going on for centuries, a simple analysis allows us to see the effects. Consider what's being done to the planet that is your present and future home: At the time of this writing, every day an estimated 60,000 industries discharge 18 billion gallons of waste water into our lakes, rivers and streams. Some 1500 new chemicals, ranging from plastics and solvents to cleaning agents and reformulated fuels enter the marketplace. Underfunded government watchdog groups check the toxicity of only about 12-20 of these substances. Fifty acres of rainforest are cut down, defoliated and burned every minute. Each year, an estimated 3.5 million tons of oil are discharged into our oceans, 85 times the volume of the Exxon Valdez spill. Every year, an area of rainforest the size of Britain is cut down or defoliated, and burnt.

These changes are not without consequence. It is estimated that about 80% of the top 150 medicines in use today are derived from plants. As the environment breaks down, the equilibrium of ecosystems that protect against the spread of viruses becomes ever more unstable. At the same time, sources of new medicines are lost forever. That's a terrible loss, because some 30 new diseases have appeared just since 1973, including AIDS, Ebola, Lyme Disease, "flesh-eating" bacteria, and two new forms of hepatitis. Since 1950, breast cancer and male colon cancer have increased by 60 percent, prostate and kidney cancers by 100 percent. 8 million Americans have cancer right now. 1.2 million new cases were diagnosed in 1997.

In light of the threat to everyone, you might think that thoughtful people would be pooling their resources and seeking solutions. Indeed, there are pockets of such activity, and their number is growing. Yet as the clock continues ticking off the moments until irreversible disaster strikes us all, special interest groups and politicians with an agenda of their own work hard to perpetuate the win/lose paradigm, promoting their own small and selfish interests over the longer term good of us all.

Here's the irony. We find consistently that when they think for themselves, people only rarely resemble the national policies and positions of their respective governments or the companies that employ them. But when individuals submerge their identities into communities of ignorance and fear, their behavior generally changes for the worst. The result is that, until now, the future of humanity has remained on the outer most fringes of our public dialogue, when instead it should be center stage with all the lights on.

SOMETHING CAN BE DONE

I do not believe in a fate that falls on men
however they act; but I do believe in a fate
that falls on them unless they act.
-Gilbert Chesterton

Yet we the people are not powerless to change our situation, to take charge over this crisis, and to turn the tide of history from the pain of the past to the incredibly great future we know is possible. Something new is occurring, and humanity is both the author of it and the witness to it. We find ourselves in a unique moment, in many ways an unprecedented moment, a moment filled with grave danger and greater opportunity than we've ever known before.

From a technical point of view, humanity now has the ability to make itself successful, to recreate our institutions and traditions so that they support the greater good rather than destroy it. Daily, you read and hear about breakthroughs in science, medicine, and technology that will alter the course of human events for generations! We now know that sunflowers remove uranium, mustard removes mercury, and corn and bermuda grass remove lead from contaminated soil. Plants can assist in the healing process for all sorts of illnesses and physical difficulties. Perhaps you're already familiar with such potent botanical remedies as St. John's Wort for depression, ginkgo for mental deterioration, and garlic for blood pressure and ginger for travel sickness.

Only a few years ago, isolating a single gene would have earned you a Nobel prize. Today, the genetic code has been cracked, and thanks to the human genome project, the structure of DNA is unraveling. A hundred new genes are found every week. The genetic foundation of intractable diseases is itself becoming vulnerable to change, while the genetic potential of cells and creatures is giving up its secrets and leading to one startling breakthrough upon another.

The buckminsterfullerene, or 'Buckyball', is a naturally occurring carbon molecule named after R. Buckminster Fuller. Bucky, as he preferred to be called, was as an architect, engineer, inventor, and philosopher, and the molecule named in his honor is as remarkable as he was. It's shape resembles the geodesic domes he pioneered, which are known for their strength, lightness, and shape. Scientists anticipate great breakthroughs with the buckyball and related molecules. There are plans to create a buckyball battery, and a whole new line of plastics. Rocket fuels, shock absorbers, and a super-strong, relatively cheap armor are other possible uses. Some scientists consider the discovery of the buckyball to be the most significant discovery of the 20th century, changing our lives for the better well into the 21st century and beyond.

Look at the big picture of these turbulent times, and the meaning of it all becomes apparent. Humanity either stands on the brink of a great catastrophe or on the threshold of a greater opportunity to bring about the success of humanity.

POINT OF VIEW

The world is my country, all mankind are my brethren, and to do good is my religion.
- Thomas Paine

A new paradigm is emerging, one that encompasses the big picture, goes beyond adversarial relationships and sees the interconnectedness of us all.

Try this simple experiment, and you can see the essence of this new paradigm for yourself. It's as plain as the nose on your face. Just put your index finger about 10 inches in front of your nose. Now close your left eye and look at your finger. Next, open your left eye and close the right. Go back and forth a few times. Do you see that finger move? Your right eye and left eye see from two different points of view. Imagine them arguing over whose point of view was correct. While that's plainly absurd, it is exactly what goes on between individuals, groups and nations all the time. Your right and left eye see from two different points of view, and each point of view is correct. When your brain puts together their two different points of view, you suddenly perceive depth and see in three dimensions. What you see is greater than the sum of the parts when taken separately. Imagine this approach applied by two people having an argument, or by two political parties in a legislature debating a hot issue, or by two countries paying the ongoing price of war. Only by understanding the value of the various points of view can something be seen that is greater than any one side. And that opens up the possibility for true solutions that address the greater good.

SPONTANEOUS COOPERATION

We cannot live only for ourselves. A thousand fibers connect us with our fellow men; and among those fibers, as sympathetic threads, our actions run as causes, and they come back to us as effects.
- Herman Melville

What's needed is something that's been missing from the picture for a long time. Something that's as timeless as a principle, and as timely as today's news. Fortunately, that something is built right into our systems. Time and again, in the aftermath of bombings, earthquakes and floods, entire communities pull themselves together into a united whole of people, meeting with and helping their neighbors cope with tragedy and loss. They do this voluntarily, and the pattern is consistent in human communities all over the world. One can only conclude that there is a principle involved. Bucky called this the principle of spontaneous cooperation. But does it have to take a tragedy for people to come together, to work together, to see the future together and then to help each other out?

In our work with various organizations, we've come to see how spontaneous cooperation is invoked without crisis and tragedy. We've seen that leadership and teamwork are two sides of the same coin. One cannot emerge without the other, and neither can be present until someone begins to elevate the vision and values and goals that speak to the greater good above the petty concerns and conflicts that render people powerless to change.

This kind of holding the focus is invaluable, yet it is only possible for you to do this if you've learned to do it for yourself first. If you want to be a part of what is changing, rather than apart from what is changing, first and foremost, you must care. To lead an initiative for change, you must care deeply for the well being of others. You must see that people are bound together by what they choose to do together. This bond is so powerful, that when it is honored and appreciated it creates a community of shared interest that generates a momentum of its own. To take the lead in your own life and live it in a meaningful way, you must have the courage to rise above pettiness and stand for something that betters the world around you.

The success of humanity, the end of hunger, war and disease, is now a choice. The key ingredient is integrity, a state of being complete, undivided and unimpaired, where actions match values, and words match deeds. In Greek, the root word for sin is 'sinus,' which means omission. The fact that our world isn't working for everybody has simply to do with the fact that not enough of us have made the success of humanity a priority, and have yet to realize that it's all of us or none of us.

IT IS YOUR CHOICE

When you have to make a choice and don't make it,
that in itself is a choice."
- William James

We the people must learn to stop polarizing over every issue, to focus our more than sufficient energy into cooperatively co-creating our collective vision of what will be. Releasing our hold on the injuries and ignorance of the past, we can take charge over our circumstances and commit the resources to solving our problems and building a sustainable future. Anything less is irresponsible, because we are all in this together. To survive, we're going to have to help each other out!

Nature can be a guide for us. Nature operates on the values of sustainability, of interconnection, of efficiency and economy. Human beings, as part of nature, must ultimately be guided by these same values. And irony of ironies, technology has at last given us the ability to discern this. Pollution is a sign of inefficiency, expensive in the long term and destructive in the big picture. Hunger and poverty are signs of inefficiency and waste as well. And war, like crime, is a battle for supremacy in a world where there isn't enough, when in fact there is more than enough for all of us if we choose a life by design for the world we share.

Clearly, nature supports both differentiation (the many) and unity (the one). Clearly, the world would benefit greatly from all of humanity with all of our diversity working together for our shared interests. But for the world to work for everyone, each of us must develop as individuals, gaining insight into our own value systems, pursuing our own visions for meaningful lives, educating ourselves with high quality information. When you follow through on the exercises in this book, when you choose to live a life by design, you add your integrity to the integrity of the system. This brings more and more of us to

222

that critical mass on the critical path of realizing that it's all of us or none of us, utopia or oblivion.

The longer we wait, the more likely it is that nature will force our hand, that we will reap the whirlwind we have sown. But if enough of us can learn as individuals to respect the honest differences between ourselves and others, to celebrate what we have in common, to define neighbor in a larger frame of reference, if we can finally figure out how to bring out the best in one another by seeing the best in another, then there is a chance for a dramatic change for the better.

A BETTER WORLD AWAITS YOUR WISDOM

Deep in my heart, I do believe.
We shall overcome someday.
- African-American hymn

Just as chemicals in the primordial soup learned to communicate and work together until they became living organisms, humanity as a whole is discovering itself, and can now become something more than it has ever been before. Thanks to technology, that brilliant byproduct of human creativity and innovation, more and more of us are now communicating with each other across the fictional boundaries by which people defined themselves in the past.

The networked world of the internet is an ideal symbol for our awakening. The network is growing fast because people organically sense the power of it and want to participate. Cooperation amongst educators, scientists, and people of diverse ethnic and religious backgrounds is on the increase. The cry for freedom and justice is more of a force in the world than ever before. And while the desire to build a better world has always been with us, our ability to bring this dream to life is now made possible in a myriad of ways unimaginable to all but the dreamers of a few short decades ago. At the same time, the power of authoritarian institutions is in decline as their inept and often corrupt nature becomes known, while the knowledge and power of the individual to make a meaningful difference is increasing rapidly.

We are finally coming to grips with a fundamental truth. We the people are in charge. And while we always have been, we seem to be losing interest in giving our power away to whomever would take it from us. We're not suggesting that suddenly there will be an end to stupidity, manipulation and bad choices. These things are also a part of the human experience. But as our options continue to multiply, more people are catching on. We stand on the threshold of a prosperous and peaceful world. Will we cross over into the promised land? That depends on our willingness to live our individual and thus collective life by design.

INVENTORY YOUR EXPERIENCE: FEEL THE HEAT

Issues Of Our Time. Take the next few minutes to write down those issues effecting the human race that you find most disturbing, the ones that make you clench your fists and grind your teeth in frustration. Write down your assumptions about these issues, and your assumptions about what it will take to resolve them. Then join us in the last chapter, to see how living your life by design changes how the world turns out.

224

22. OWNING THE WORLD

DON'T JUST SIT THERE!

It is by acts and not by ideas that people live.
-Anatole France

We hope that we've provided you with evidence throughout the preceding chapters that it is possible to design your life and live your life by that design. The rest is up to you. But the nature of our times presses in and you must see that your presence on earth has value and significance in the larger tapestry of life. What is the world that you imagine when you consider a world that works? Please take a close look. What does that mean to you? Do you have a compelling vision of the future pulling you forward?

We envision a world where color, culture, age and intelligence are recognized as part of the diversity of nature. Where there is no hunger, because the bottom line is covered for everyone. Where having clean air and water are a priority, and technology is used to keep it that way. And we're not alone in these dreams of what is possible. We hear similar visions from people all over the world, from our elders and our children, from our neighbors. In such dreaming, people are more alike than they are different. If together we aim our collective vision of the possible, we can break free from the inertia of a mixed up world and leave a great message for the future about who we were, what we did, and what we valued.

We've also been listening to people expressing their ideas about how we will find our way into the future. Some say that a great person will appear, or a tragic event will occur, a world government will form or humanity will muddle through until the cost of ignorance is too great. Each of these scenarios conveniently places the responsibility for the future on someone else, everybody else, anyone else. But as far as we can tell, you are the one on whom your future depends right now. And the possibility exists that the future of the world depends on you.

We have a theory about leadership. We call it the great moment theory, and it goes like this. Isn't this a great moment? After all, this is the pivotal moment upon which all change will occur. This is the moment of action, today is the first day of the rest of your life, the past is available here and now to learn from, the future is available here and now to design and influence.

It has been said that leadership is the wise use of power. Taking the lead in your life is possible if you use the power available to you in this moment to follow through. What power are we referring to?

George Bernard Shaw wrote:

"This is the true joy in life, the being used for a purpose recognized by yourself as a mighty one; the being a force of nature instead of a feverish selfish little clod of ailments and grievances complaining that the world will not devote itself to making you happy. I want to be thoroughly used up when I die, for the harder I work the more I live. I rejoice in life for its own sake. Life is no "brief candle" to me.

It is a sort of splendid torch which I have got hold of for the moment , and I want to make it burn as brightly as possible before handing it on to future generations."

A community, a state, a country, indeed the world is just the sum total of the hopes and dreams, fears and grudges, beliefs and assumptions of its people. So the best and most direct way to change the world must be to change yourself, to lead the world by leading yourself. Because if you can't change your own warring ways and im- poverished behavior, then the collective result has one more problem person adding to the burden of the problem.

Here's a recipe for recovery, renewal and regeneration of life on planet Earth that starts with you.

Get your own house in order.

Take the time to use what you've learned, in this book and else- where, to cultivate a sense of vision and clarity about your values until you feel connected to how your life turns out.

Take some time To feel alive.

There is no time like the present, ever! Only through apprecia- tion of the good in your life right now can you keep your mind and heart clear and courageous enough to face the challenges of life on earth.

End hunger by nourishing yourself.

The root word for nourishment means 'to cherish.' There is already enough hunger in the world. Feed your head with uplifting and inspiring words and ideas. Draw freely from the well of your ancestors, as their hopes and dreams gave birth to your heart's desires. Feed your spirit with the eternal, the sublime and the transcendent in order to overcome the muddiness and negativity caused by the daily bombardments of global stupidity.

See The World As Your Reflection

When John Lennon told us that "War is over, if you want it," he wasn't referring to this political conflict or that ethnic strife. He was talking about all the world and the condition of irresponsibility that makes war an option. End the wars within yourself and between yourself and others. Forgiveness of your own shortcomings and the failings and foibles of others will free up your mental and emotional energy for your creative use.

End the pollution by cleaning up your act.

The slow and certain destruction of the mind and body that results from bad choices about food, drink, activity and surroundings is one dimension of the pollution problem. But just like too much of a bad thing can be bad for your health, too much of a good thing can be harmful too! There's no need to become a fanatic. Moderation is a better thing. You have more than enough information about how to eat right, how to take time for a little R&R, and how to break bad habits and replace them with life enhancing behavior. You don't have to be perfect. You just have to begin to be balanced and wise, and grow in your wisdom through time.

Treat Yourself And Others With Respect

Life is not cheap. It has tremendous value. By strengthening your respect for all of life, you add value to it. By using your unique inventory of experience in service to others, you add their value to yourself.

Give What You Have In Abundance

We're all a little different, maybe some more than others. None of us can be everything to everyone, but all of us can be who we are and do something for someone. Wherever your cup runneth over, that's the place to put more cups and share whatever it is that you have more than enough of. It may be time, money, energy, talent, networking, service work, speaking other languages! Everybody is given more than they need of something, and getting it off the shelf and into service makes all the difference in the world.

End the ignorance by educating yourself.

In the distant past, all human knowledge tended to be centralized in one easy to conquer and destroy location. Today, educating yourself is now easier than ever before, thanks to the ready availability of the internet, libraries, personal computers, books, tapes and other materials. What you don't know can hurt you, and education is a ready shield. Educate yourself about the issues of our time, then find people who share your convictions and share this information with them. As the circle of knowledge expands, ignorance must retreat.

The World Is Waiting Just For You

If I am not for myself, who will be for me? And if I am only for myself, what am I? And if not now, when?
- Hillel

The human experience was designed with plenty of time and space for us to make foolish choices and still continue on. But it's entirely possible that we've arrived at the end of the womb of acceptable ignorance. Like waking up in the passenger seat of a car heading for a cliff and discovering that there's nobody behind the wheel, we now have a choice: Do we leave it on cruise control or get in the driver's seat and steer our way to safety?

We the people, in order to create a more perfect union, must tear down the walls of our own construction, dance on the rubble of what was, seize the moment to build what will be in service to the greater good. You can be the one who chooses to help the miracles unfold. The solutions are all around you. The choices are yours. In more ways than one, this is the future, and humanity has the same choice that you do: A life by default, or a life by design. We have great faith in you.

ABOUT THE AUTHORS

Dr. Rick Kirschner and Dr. Rick Brinkman are the coauthors of the McGraw Hill international bestseller, 'Dealing With People You Can't Stand: How To Bring Out The Best In People At Their Worst,' the bestselling audio and video program 'How To Deal With Difficult People,' the award-winning Athena Interactive CD-Rom, 'Dealing With Difficult People, the customer service training video and audio program 'Telecare,' and the book for getting everyone in an organization on the same page about service, 'Love Thy Customer.'

They speak to audiences across the nation and around the world on the subjects of change, communication, conflict resolution, persuasion and service excellence. Their client portfolio includes many of the Fortune 1000 companies, hundreds of small and medium sized business, government agencies, healthcare facilities and professional associations.

Their unique presentation style of 'Educating Through Entertainment,' includes stand-up comedy, hard-hitting stories, and dramatic skits. Rick and Rick have earned the goodwill and trust of leaders in industry, education, healthcare and government. They provide a wide range of resources to individuals and organizations in pursuit of excellence.

For information on bringing either of the Ricks to your organization:

Dr. Brinkman   http://RickBrinkman.com

Dr. Kirschner   http://TheArtofChange.com

The American Association of Naturopathic Physicians

http://naturopathic.org

THE ARTIST

Graphics by Les Hopkins

Invitation From The Authors

We would love to hear from you, whether to share your success stories, find out about our books and tapes, or to request our availability for a speaking engagement.

We invite you to contact us:

for Dr. Brinkman: dr.rick@rickbrinkman.com

for Dr. Kirschner: DrKInfo@TheArtofChange.com

87817195R00126

Made in the USA
Columbia, SC
27 January 2018